Funny in
Farsi

Funny in Farsi

A Memoir of
Growing Up Iranian
in America

FIROOZEH DUMAS

VILLARD NEW YORK Ⓥ

All rights reserved under International and Pan-American Copyright Conventions. Published in the United States by Villard Books, an imprint of The Random House Publishing Group, a division of Random House, Inc., New York, and simultaneously in Canada by Random House of Canada Limited, Toronto.

VILLARD and "V" CIRCLED Design are registered trademarks of Random House, Inc.

Library of Congress Cataloging-in-Publication Data
Dumas, Firoozeh.
    Funny in Farsi : a memoir of growing up Iranian in America / Firoozeh Dumas.
        p.   cm.
    ISBN 1-4000-6040-0 (acid-free paper)
    1. Dumas, Firoozeh. 2. Iranian American women—Biography. 3. Iranian Americans—Biography. 4. Immigrants—United States—Biography. 5. Dumas, Firoozeh—Family. 6. Abadan (Iran)—Biography. 7. Whittier (Calif.)—Biography. 8. United States—Social life and customs—1972–
I. Title.
    E184.15 D86   2003
    979.4'90049155'0092—dc21   2002034921

Villard Books website address: www.villard.com

Printed in the United States of America on acid-free paper

9876543

Designed by Cassandra J. Pappas

To my father, Kazem,
who loves to tell stories.

And to my mother, Nazireh.

ACKNOWLEDGMENTS

My thanks to Bonnie Nadell for taking a chance on an unknown, for the title, and for always being a pleasant voice on the other end of the line; to everyone at Villard Books, in particular my talented editor, Bruce Tracy, whose intuition, fine-tuning skills, and great laugh made this a dream project; to F.D., N.K., and S.M. for making my heart sing; to L.P., C.K., K.K., and the Thursday hiking group for showing me that all hills must be climbed in the company of friends; and to my relatives, all of whom laugh without an accent, *merci*.

CONTENTS

Funny in Farsi

Leffingwell Elementary School

When I was seven, my parents, my fourteen-year-old brother, Farshid, and I moved from Abadan, Iran, to Whittier, California. Farid, the older of my two brothers, had been sent to Philadelphia the year before to attend high school. Like most Iranian youths, he had always dreamed of attending college abroad and, despite my mother's tears, had left us to live with my uncle and his American wife. I, too, had been sad at Farid's departure, but my sorrow soon faded—not coincidentally, with the receipt of a package from him. Suddenly, having my brother on a different continent seemed like a small price to pay for owning a Barbie complete with a carrying case and four outfits, including the rain gear and mini umbrella.

Our move to Whittier was temporary. My father, Kazem, an engineer with the National Iranian Oil Company, had been assigned to consult for an American firm for about two years. Having spent several years in Texas and California as a graduate student, my father often spoke about America with the eloquence and wonder normally reserved for a first love. To him, America was a place where anyone, no matter how humble his

3

background, could become an important person. It was a kind and orderly nation full of clean bathrooms, a land where traffic laws were obeyed and where whales jumped through hoops. It was the Promised Land. For me, it was where I could buy more outfits for Barbie.

We arrived in Whittier shortly after the start of second grade; my father enrolled me in Leffingwell Elementary School. To facilitate my adjustment, the principal arranged for us to meet my new teacher, Mrs. Sandberg, a few days before I started school. Since my mother and I did not speak English, the meeting consisted of a dialogue between my father and Mrs. Sandberg. My father carefully explained that I had attended a prestigious kindergarten where all the children were taught English. Eager to impress Mrs. Sandberg, he asked me to demonstrate my knowledge of the English language. I stood up straight and proudly recited all that I knew: "White, yellow, orange, red, purple, blue, green."

The following Monday, my father drove my mother and me to school. He had decided that it would be a good idea for my mother to attend school with me for a few weeks. I could not understand why two people not speaking English would be better than one, but I was seven, and my opinion didn't matter much.

Until my first day at Leffingwell Elementary School, I had never thought of my mother as an embarrassment, but the sight of all the kids in the school staring at us before the bell rang was enough to make me pretend I didn't know her. The bell finally rang and Mrs. Sandberg came and escorted us to class. Fortunately, she had figured out that we were precisely the kind of people who would need help finding the right classroom.

My mother and I sat in the back while all the children took their assigned seats. Everyone continued to stare at us. Mrs. Sandberg wrote my name on the board: F-I-R-O-O-Z-E-H.

Under my name, she wrote "I-R-A-N." She then pulled down a map of the world and said something to my mom. My mom looked at me and asked me what she had said. I told her that the teacher probably wanted her to find Iran on the map.

The problem was that my mother, like most women of her generation, had been only briefly educated. In her era, a girl's sole purpose in life was to find a husband. Having an education ranked far below more desirable attributes such as the ability to serve tea or prepare baklava. Before her marriage, my mother, Nazireh, had dreamed of becoming a midwife. Her father, a fairly progressive man, had even refused the two earlier suitors who had come for her so that his daughter could pursue her dream. My mother planned to obtain her diploma, then go to Tabriz to learn midwifery from a teacher whom my grandfather knew. Sadly, the teacher died unexpectedly, and my mother's dreams had to be buried as well.

Bachelor No. 3 was my father. Like the other suitors, he had never spoken to my mother, but one of his cousins knew someone who knew my mother's sister, so that was enough. More important, my mother fit my father's physical requirements for a wife. Like most Iranians, my father preferred a fair-skinned woman with straight, light-colored hair. Having spent a year in America as a Fulbright scholar, he had returned with a photo of a woman he found attractive and asked his older sister, Sedigeh, to find someone who resembled her. Sedigeh had asked around, and that is how at age seventeen my mother officially gave up her dreams, married my father, and had a child by the end of the year.

As the students continued staring at us, Mrs. Sandberg gestured to my mother to come up to the board. My mother reluctantly obeyed. I cringed. Mrs. Sandberg, using a combination of hand gestures, started pointing to the map and saying, "Iran?

Iran? Iran?" Clearly, Mrs. Sandberg had planned on incorporating us into the day's lesson. I only wished she had told us that earlier so we could have stayed home.

After a few awkward attempts by my mother to find Iran on the map, Mrs. Sandberg finally understood that it wasn't my mother's lack of English that was causing a problem, but rather her lack of world geography. Smiling graciously, she pointed my mother back to her seat. Mrs. Sandberg then showed everyone, including my mother and me, where Iran was on the map. My mother nodded her head, acting as if she had known the location all along but had preferred to keep it a secret. Now all the students stared at us, not just because I had come to school with my mother, not because we couldn't speak their language, but because we were stupid. I was especially mad at my mother, because she had negated the positive impression I had made previously by reciting the color wheel. I decided that starting the next day, *she* would have to stay home.

The bell finally rang and it was time for us to leave. Leffingwell Elementary was just a few blocks from our house and my father, grossly underestimating our ability to get lost, had assumed that my mother and I would be able to find our way home. She and I wandered aimlessly, perhaps hoping for a shooting star or a talking animal to help guide us back. None of the streets or houses looked familiar. As we stood pondering our predicament, an enthusiastic young girl came leaping out of her house and said something. Unable to understand her, we did what we had done all day: we smiled. The girl's mother joined us, then gestured for us to follow her inside. I assumed that the girl, who appeared to be the same age as I, was a student at Leffingwell Elementary; having us inside her house was probably akin to having the circus make a personal visit.

Her mother handed us a telephone, and my mother, who had, thankfully, memorized my father's work number, called him and explained our situation. My father then spoke to the American woman and gave her our address. This kind stranger agreed to take us back to our house.

Perhaps fearing that we might show up at their doorstep again, the woman and her daughter walked us all the way to our front porch and even helped my mother unlock the unfamiliar door. After making one last futile attempt at communication, they waved good-bye. Unable to thank them in words, we smiled even more broadly.

After spending an entire day in America, surrounded by Americans, I realized that my father's description of America had been correct. The bathrooms were clean and the people were very, very kind.

Hot Dogs and Wild Geese

Moving to America was both exciting and frightening, but we found great comfort in knowing that my father spoke English. Having spent years regaling us with stories about his graduate years in America, he had left us with the distinct impression that America was his second home. My mother and I planned to stick close to him, letting him guide us through the exotic American landscape that he knew so well. We counted on him not only to translate the language but also to translate the culture, to be a link to this most foreign of lands. He was to be our own private Rosetta stone.

Once we reached America, we wondered whether perhaps my father had confused his life in America with someone else's. Judging from the bewildered looks of store cashiers, gas station attendants, and waiters, my father spoke a version of English not yet shared with the rest of America. His attempts to find a "vater closet" in a department store would usually lead us to the drinking fountain or the home furnishings section. Asking my father to ask the waitress the definition of "sloppy Joe" or "Tater Tots" was no problem. His translations, however, were highly suspect.

Waitresses would spend several minutes responding to my father's questions, and these responses, in turn, would be translated as "She doesn't know." Thanks to my father's translations, we stayed away from hot dogs, catfish, and hush puppies, and no amount of caviar in the sea would have convinced us to try mud pie.

We wondered how my father had managed to spend several years attending school in America yet remain so utterly befuddled by Americans. We soon discovered that his college years had been spent mainly in the library, where he had managed to avoid contact with all Americans except his engineering professors. As long as the conversation was limited to vectors, surface tension, and fluid mechanics, my father was Fred Astaire with words. But one step outside the scintillating world of petroleum engineering and he had two left tongues.

My father's only other regular contact in college had been his roommate, a Pakistani who spent his days preparing curry. Since neither spoke English but both liked curries, they got along splendidly. The person who had assigned them together had probably hoped they would either learn English or invent a common language for the occasion. Neither happened.

My father's inability to understand spoken English was matched only by his efforts to deny the problem. His constant attempts at communicating with Americans seemed at first noble and adventurous, then annoying. Somewhere between his thick Persian accent and his use of vocabulary found in pre–World War II British textbooks, my father spoke a private language. That nobody understood him hurt his pride, so what he lacked in speaking ability, he made up for by reading. He was the only person who actually read each and every document before he signed it. Buying a washing machine from Sears might take the average American thirty minutes, but by the time my father had finished reading the warranties, terms of contracts, and credit information, the store was closing and the janitor was asking us to please step aside so he could finish mopping the floor.

My mother's approach to learning English consisted of daily lessons with Monty Hall and Bob Barker. Her devotion to *Let's Make a Deal* and *The Price Is Right* was evident in her newfound ability to recite useless information. After a few months of television viewing, she could correctly tell us whether a coffeemaker cost more or less than $19.99. How many boxes of Hamburger Helper, Swanson's TV dinners, or Turtle Wax could one buy without spending a penny more than twenty dollars? She knew that, too. Strolling down the grocery aisle, she rejoiced in her celebrity sightings—Lipton tea! Campbell's tomato soup! Betty Crocker Rich & Creamy Frosting! Every day, she would tell us the day's wins and losses on the game shows. "He almost won the boat, but the wife picked curtain number two and they ended up with a six-foot chicken statue." The bad prizes on *Let's Make a Deal* sounded far more intriguing than the good ones. Who would want the matching La-Z-Boy recliners when they could have the adult-size crib and high-chair set?

My mother soon decided that the easiest way for her to communicate with Americans was to use me as an interpreter. My brother Farshid, with his schedule full of soccer, wrestling, and karate, was too busy to be recruited for this dubious honor. At an age when most parents are guiding their kids toward independence, my mother was hanging on to me for dear life. I had to accompany her to the grocery store, the hairdresser, the doctor, and every place else that a kid wouldn't want to go. My reward for doing this was the constant praise of every American we encountered. Hearing a seven-year-old translate Persian into English and vice versa made quite an impression on everyone. People lavished compliments on me. "You must be very, very smart, a genius maybe." I always responded by assuring them that if they ever moved to another country, they, too, would learn the language. (What I wanted to say was that I wished I could be at home watching *The Brady Bunch* instead of translating the qualities of various facial moisturizers.) My mother had her own response to the compliments: "Americans are easily impressed."

I always encouraged my mother to learn English, but her talents lay elsewhere. Since she had never learned English in school, she had no idea of its grammar. She would speak entire paragraphs without using any verbs. She referred to everyone and everything as "it," leaving the listener wondering whether she was talking about her husband or the kitchen table. Even if she did speak a sentence more or less correctly, her accent made it incomprehensible. "W" and "th" gave her the most difficulty. As if God were playing a linguistic joke on us, we lived in "Vee-tee-er" (Whittier), we shopped at "Veetvood" (Whitwood) Plaza, I attended "Leffingvell" School, and our neighbor was none other than "Valter Villiams."

Despite little progress on my mother's part, I continually encouraged her. Rather than teach her English vocabulary and grammar, I eventually decided to teach her entire sentences to repeat. I assumed that once she got used to speaking correctly, I could be removed, like training wheels, and she would continue coasting. I was wrong.

Noticing some insects in our house one day, my mother asked me to call the exterminator. I looked up the number, then told my mother to call and say, "We have silverfish in our house." My mother grumbled, dialed the number, and said, "Please come rrright a-vay. Goldfeeesh all over dee house." The exterminator told her he'd be over as soon as he found his fishing pole.

A few weeks later, our washing machine broke. A repairman was summoned and the leaky pipe was quickly replaced. My mother wanted to know how to remove the black stain left by the leak. "Y'all are gonna hafta use some elbow grease," he said. I thanked him and paid him and walked with my mother to the hardware store. After searching fruitlessly for elbow grease, I asked the salesclerk for help. "It removes stains," I added. The manager was called.

Once the manager finished laughing, he gave us the disappointing explanation. My mother and I walked home empty-handed. That, I later learned, is what Americans call a wild-goose chase.

Now that my parents have lived in America for thirty years, their English has improved somewhat, but not as much as one would hope. It's not entirely their fault; English is a confusing language. When my father paid his friend's daughter the compliment of calling her homely, he meant she would be a great housewife. When he complained about horny drivers, he was referring to their tendency to honk. And my parents still don't understand why teenagers want to be cool so they can be hot.

I no longer encourage my parents to learn English. I've given up. Instead, I'm grateful for the wave of immigration that has brought Iranian television, newspapers, and supermarkets to America. Now, when my mother wants to ask the grocer whether he has any more eggplants in the back that are a little darker and more firm, because the ones he has out aren't right for *khoresht bademjun,* she can do so in Persian, all by herself. And for that, I say hallelujah, a word that needs no translation.

In the Gutter

My father grew up poor in Ahwaz, Iran. His parents died at an early age, brought down by maladies readily cured today. He and his siblings survived through teamwork, and now, even though they are well into their seventies and have many kids and grandkids, they remain the central players in one another's lives. They have supported one another through deaths and illnesses and rejoiced in one another's good fortune. If someone were to ask my father about his proudest moment, he would probably mention the day his nephew Muhammad finally bought a house in America, or the day his great-nephew Mahan graduated from law school. Telling my father that his beloved older sister, Sedigeh, is angry with him is like putting a grown man in time out. He just can't stand it. The unbreakable bond between my father and his siblings serves as a testimonial that even though their parents lived very short lives, they did something right.

My father's hardscrabble life also left him with a burning desire to get rich. History is full of stories of men overcoming poverty to amass great fortunes in steel or pig farming. Others reach great heights through education, becoming successful doctors and lawyers. My father was an educated man, but as a salaried engineer, he had not a chance of becoming rich, and he knew it. Unwilling to abandon his champagne wishes and caviar dreams, my father dreamed of ways to get rich that required neither hard work nor further education. His dream was that the doorbell would ring and he would answer it. Standing there would be a man in a three-piece navy blue suit who would ask him, "Are you Kazem?"

"Yes," my father would answer.

Then the man would inform my father that through a series of unbelievable circumstances, he had come into boatloads of money.

It was with this mind-set that my father decided to enter *Bowling for Dollars*.

In his attempts to embrace American culture, my father had joined the local bowling league. Every Wednesday evening, he would head off to the bowling alley, returning with spellbinding stories about strikes and gutters. Somewhere along the way, he started to believe that he was a gifted bowler. I suspect it had something to do with the American habit of generously heaping praise and encouragement on anyone who tries anything. At some point, someone must have yelled "Good job, Kaz!," which my father interpreted as "You should go on television and win a fortune!"

Bowling for Dollars was a game show that merged the fascinating world of bowling with the thrill of Las Vegas. All a contestant had to do to win the jackpot was roll two strikes in a row. The jackpot grew each time a contestant failed to win, taking the excitement up a notch. My parents and I watched the show religiously, with my father's running commentary, which did not resemble that of traditional sports announcers, in the background. My father's comments ranged from "You should've gotten that!" to "I would've gotten that!" From our sofa, bowling looked easy, and we couldn't understand why so many contestants failed to win the jackpot. At the end of each show, viewers were encouraged to call the studio to become a contestant. My father gathered the courage to call and was invited to come for a trial run.

Like a bride preparing to walk down the aisle, my father carefully chose his clothing, got a haircut, and practiced saying "Hello, I am Kazem" to the bathroom mirror. My mother, now a self-declared bowling expert, gave him all kinds of advice. "Make sure you win."

My father drove the hour-and-a-half round-trip to the Burbank studio for the first trial run and returned feeling triumphant. He hadn't bowled any strikes, but he had been asked to return for the second practice. If the second practice went well, he would then appear on television.

Another hour-and-a-half trip for the second practice, and he was selected to return for a taping of the show. My father was hoping that none of the contestants before him would win, so that the jackpot would be really big. He didn't want to merely win the jackpot; he wanted to win a huge one.

The big day finally arrived and my father was ready to strike it rich. He filled the Impala with gas and set off for the third and final drive to the studio. We waited anxiously at home.

My father returned that night looking sadder than I had ever seen him. In his two tries, he had hit a total of only seven pins, winning seven dollars. He had never before bowled so poorly. He blamed his poor performance on everything from the lights to the long drive. We didn't care why he hadn't won; we just could not recall anybody winning so little on *Bowling for Dollars*. My father had spent several times as much on gasoline just driving back and forth to the studio.

When the performance was aired a few weeks after the taping, we watched in silence. My father looked very nervous on television, especially after he hit his first gutter ball. After the second gutter ball, he looked positively panicked.

After this brush with fame, we no longer watched *Bowling for Dollars*. We didn't feel the same emotional involvement. Who were we to criticize these people, all of whom managed to win more than seven dollars?

Shortly thereafter, my father gave up bowling entirely, deciding it was a stupid sport, if one could even call it a sport. More important, his Wednesday evening bowling nights had forced him to miss *The Sonny and Cher Comedy Hour*. Now he was able to squeeze onto the sofa with the rest of us and catch up.

Save Me, Mickey

When we first came to America in 1972, we knew we would be staying only for about two years. This gave us approximately 104 weekends to see everything there was to see in California. From Knott's Berry Farm to Marine World, from the Date Festival to the Garlic Festival, we saw it all. Along the way, we tasted garlic ice cream, date shakes, and cherry slushies, and other foods that we no longer remember, although we do recall the ensuing scrambles to the drugstore for Rolaids.

Because we were new to this country, we were impressed not just by the big attractions but also by the little things—smiling employees, clean bathrooms, and clear signage. Our ability to be impressed by the large selection of key chains at the souvenir shops guaranteed that every place we saw delighted us.

There was, however, one attraction that stood apart, one whose sweatshirts we wore with pride, one that generated near religious devotion: Disneyland. My father believed that Walt Disney was a genius, a man whose vision allowed everyone, regardless of age, to relive the wonderment of childhood. Ask my father what he considers to be man's greatest creation in the twentieth century and he won't say computers, the Concorde, or knee replacement surgery. For him, "Pirates of the Caribbean" represents the pinnacle of man's creative achievement. No matter how many times my father goes on that ride, he remains as impressed as a Disneyland virgin. "Did you see that pirate leg hanging over the bridge? Could somebody remind me that it wasn't real? And the battle between the ships, geez, was I the only one ready to duck and cover? What kind of a man would think of creating something like this? A genius, that's who." I doubt that even Walt Disney's mother felt as much pride in her son as my father did.

According to my father, any activity that is enjoyed by our family will be exponentially more enjoyable if shared with others. A crowded dinner at his sister's house where only half the guests have chairs is preferred to a meal with four people and ample seating. His tribal nature may result from having grown up with eight siblings, but whatever the root cause, my father decided that if Disneyland was fun for our family, just think how much more fun it would be with twenty other people. That is how one weekend we found ourselves at Disneyland's main entrance with six of my father's Iranian colleagues and their families.

I had already been to Disneyland fifteen times and was, frankly, getting a little sick of the place. I knew every turn in every ride and all the punch lines to all the shows. But nonetheless, on yet another Saturday morning, I stood in front of Mr. Toad's Wild Ride with a large group of people, all oohing and aahing, as my father, the self-appointed ambassador to the Magic Kingdom, pointed out fascinating tidbits: "See how people just wait patiently in these long lines? In other countries, you'd have a fight! But not here, this is America."

We roamed through Disneyland like a herd of buffalo, stopping only at the rides deemed worthy by my father. At one point, we found ourselves near the telephones where one could talk to Mickey Mouse. As my father was busy explaining the wonders of the nearby Monsanto ride with the big eyeball that looks positively real, I decided to experiment with the phones, which I had somehow never tried before. I picked up the receiver and discovered that there was no conversation with Mickey Mouse on these so-called phones, just a taped message. Disgruntled, I hung up and looked around to find the rest of the herd. They were gone.

One of my father's biggest fears in moving to America was child kidnappings. Our hometown, Abadan, was about as safe a place as one could hope for. We knew all the neighbors, everyone looked out for everyone else's kids, and there was basically no crime other than petty theft. Whenever my relatives came to visit us in America, they would watch the evening news a few times, and then refuse to leave the house. "It's too dangerous here," they always said. "Why are there so many shootings?" In Iran, citizens do not have access to guns, so we do not have the types of crimes that so often lead to murders in America. My father was acutely aware of the dangers inherent in our new surroundings and lectured me regularly on the perils of strangers and how I should always go to the police if I ever needed help.

There were no police officers in Disneyland, so instead I opted for the young man in the powder blue jumpsuit wearing the hat that resembled an inverted origami boat. "I'm lost," I told him. "Okay," he said in a kind voice. "Can you tell me what your par-

ents look like?" I told him. "Now can you tell me what your parents are wearing?" he asked. No seven-year-old, except maybe a
young Giorgio Armani, could tell you what his parents were
wearing on a given day.

After my failure to answer the clothing question, Mr. Poly-
ester escorted me to a small building near the main entrance.
This was the Lost and Found, a place that, not surprisingly, I had
never noticed during my previous visits. Once I entered the
room, I started to cry. Several women surrounded me and asked
me my name, which I, in the midst of my mucus-choked sobs,
had to repeat several times. "What kind of a name is that?" one
of them asked. It was as if I was doomed to answer the same questions over and over again, for the rest of my life.

"I'm from Iran," I sniffled.

"How nice," she said. From the look on her face, I could tell
she had no idea where that was. Another one complimented me
on my English. Then they told me not to worry. I could just sit
down here and color while I waited for my parents to come and
get me. I continued to cry. The three women tried to comfort
me, but by then I had decided to cry the whole time.

A few minutes later, the door opened and in came a screaming
boy who looked to be a few years younger than I. As Team Comfort rushed to his side, it became apparent that this boy spoke
no English. No matter what the women said to him, he just
screamed. When asked his name, he shook his head and cried
louder. In desperation, one of the employees turned around and
started walking toward me with a big I-have-a-great-idea smile
on her face. I knew what was coming. "Is that boy from your
country?" she asked me. "Why, yes," I wanted to tell her. "In my
country, which I own, this is National Lose Your Child at Disneyland Day."

"No," I told her. "He's not from my country." I had no idea where the screamer was from, but I knew he wasn't Iranian. A gerbil would never mistake a hamster for a gerbil, and I would never mistake a non-Iranian for an Iranian. Despite the belief of most Westerners that all Middle Easterners look alike, we can pick each other out of a crowd as easily as my Japanese friends pick out their own from a crowd of Asians. It's like we have a certain radio frequency that only other Iranian radars pick up.

After a few futile attempts to communicate with the boy, another one of the women came to me and asked me if I could please, in my language, ask that boy his name. I told her that I spoke Persian and I was certain that the boy did not. The woman then knelt down and got real close to my face, skills picked up during Coercion 101. Speaking very slowly, she told me that she needed me to do her a favor. I could tell she was trying to remember my name. She was thinking hard. "Sweetie," she finally said, choosing to sidestep the name like a soldier avoiding a land mine, "could you just *try* to talk to him? Will you do it for Mickey?"

I wanted to tell her that Mickey was the reason I was lost in the first place. Had I not been trying to talk to him on those so-called phones, I wouldn't be sitting here. I didn't owe that rodent anything.

I once again told her that I spoke Persian and I could just tell that the boy did not. "Could you just try?" she pleaded.

Just to get rid of her, I walked up to the boy, who, breaking all stamina records, was still crying, and said in Persian, "Are you Iranian?" The boy stopped crying for a moment, then let out the loudest scream heard since biblical times. Not only was he separated from his loved ones, he was now trapped in the Tower of Babel.

Although I was sorry for the little boy, I also felt vindicated. I went back to my coloring book, no longer feeling the urge to cry. I colored a few pages; then, lo and behold, in walked my father, looking completely panicked and breathless. He ran and hugged me and asked me whether I had cried. "Of course not," I answered. He told me that I had gotten lost just when the group split in two, so an hour went by before anyone noticed I was missing. "I thought you had been kidnapped," he told me, still out of breath. Timing is key, and I knew this was my moment. "Could we go to the gift shop?" I asked. "Anything you want," he said, "anything at all."

We had to leave Disneyland early that day because my father was too weak in the knees to continue. Even the thought of "Pirates of the Caribbean" could not revive him.

We spent the usual half hour looking for our car in the parking lot. I clutched closely two helium balloons, items my father prior to this visit had always called a waste of money and never bought for me, a two-foot-long pencil with scenes from Disneyland, a complete set of miniature plastic Seven Dwarves with their own carrying case, and a Winnie-the-Pooh pencil holder. In the midst of my father's newfound appreciation for me, I also asked him if he would take me to the Movieland Wax Museum the following week. "Sure," he said. "Anything you want."

My father spent the drive home re-creating my actions in his absence.

"So how did you know for sure you were lost?" he asked.

"I couldn't see you guys," I answered.

"How did you know whom to go to?" he continued.

"I looked for someone who worked there."

"How did you know he worked there and he wasn't just standing around looking for lost kids?"

"He had the same outfit as the other six people around him and he had a name tag."

"A name tag, huh? Very clever."

I knew what he was thinking. Thanks to Mickey, I had been elevated from child-who-can't-learn-to-swim to child genius.

The following weekend, standing in the Movieland Wax Museum gift shop, I was having a hard time deciding among the visor, the inflatable mini pool with the museum logo, and the deck of cards emblazoned with four different movie stars. Then I heard my father utter the magic phrase "Why don't we just get all of them?" "Good idea," I said, hoping his newly generous view of useless purchases was more than a passing phase.

We left the gift shop with my father holding firmly on to my hand, just as he had done the entire day. Clutching my purchases with my other hand, I basked in my new status as favorite child. Perhaps I did owe that rodent something.

Swoosh-Swoosh

Every family has a daredevil. In my father's family, the honor goes to Uncle Nematollah, whose daring feat consisted of selecting his own wives, three times.

Marriage, in my culture, has nothing to do with romance. It's a matter of logic. If Mr. and Mrs. Ahmadi like Mr. and Mrs. Nejati, then their children should get married. On the other hand, if the parents don't like each other, but the children do, well, this is where sad poetry comes from. As odd as these logical unions may appear to the Western world, their success rate is probably no worse than that of marriages based on eyes meeting across a crowded room and the heart going va-va-va-boom.

After my uncle's second divorce, he decided to take a break from his medical practice in Ahwaz and come visit us in Whittier. For my American friends, "a visiting relative" meant a three-night stay. In my family, relatives' stays were marked by seasons, not nights. No one bothered coming halfway around the world for just the month of December. Might as well stay to experience spring in California, the children's graduation ceremonies in June, and Halloween. It didn't matter that our house was barely big enough for us. My father's motto has always been "Room in the heart, room in the house." As charming as this sounds, it translates into a long line for the bathroom and extra loads of laundry for my mother.

My father and his younger brother, Nematollah, share many interests, none stronger than the love of new foods. Some experience a foreign land through museums or historical sights, but for our family, America was to be experienced through the taste buds. Every day, Kazem and Nematollah, like cavemen headed for the hunt, would drive to the local supermarket, returning with cans and boxes of mysterious American products. They picked foods for the pictures on the containers, inadvertently proving that American marketing is sometimes better than American cooking. Since Iranian flavors are quite different from the flavors found in American convenience foods, most of the purchases ended up in the trash can.

In Iran, meal preparation took up half of each day, starting early in the morning with my mother telling our servant, Zahra, which vegetables to clean and cut. The vegetables were either grown in our garden or had been purchased the day before. The ingredients in our meals were limited to what was in season. Summer meant eggplant or okra stew, fresh tomatoes, and tiny cucumbers that I would peel and salt. Winter meant celery or rhubarb stew, cilantro, parsley, fenugreek, and my favorite fruit, sweet lemon, which is a thin-skinned, aromatic citrus not found in America. There was no such thing as canned, frozen, or fast food. Everything, except for bread, which was purchased daily, was made from scratch. Eating meant having to wait for hours for all the ingredients to blend together just right. When the meal was finally ready, we all sat together and savored the sensuous experience of a delicious Persian meal. Upscale restaurants in

America, calling themselves "innovative and gourmet," prepare food the way we used to. In Iran, it was simply how everybody ate.

As Zahra began frying the onions and vegetables each morning, delicious smells wafted through our house. She and her husband, Ali, who was our gardener, lived in a small house on our property. Unlike America, where only the very wealthy have live-in servants, in Iran even middle-class families employ full-time help. Ali and Zahra were from a small village in northern Iran; with us, they could earn more money than was possible back home. They were very happy, and even though my parents found them another family to live with, no one cried harder than they did when we moved to America.

After several weeks of trying every TV dinner, canned good, and cereal, my father and uncle concluded that the only ready-made American foods worth buying were canned chili, ice cream, and Chips Ahoy cookies. The rest, they concluded, was too salty, too sweet, or just plain bad.

They next set out to explore the unknown territory of American fast food. We lived near a strip mall well supplied with restaurants, all of which took a similar high-grease approach to cooking. Starting at one end, we ate our way through the mall, skipping only a hot dog place called Der Wienerschnitzel. The name was unpronounceable and we had no interest in dogs, hot or otherwise.

After weeks of research, we concluded that Kentucky Fried Chicken was the best thing we had tasted in America, followed by Baskin-Robbins, every last one of its flavors. No one was made happier by our foray into eating prepared foods than my mother, who, lacking both Iranian ingredients and Zahra, had a very difficult time cooking in America. The Colonel's secret recipe had set my mother free.

Several times a week, my father would buy a couple of buckets of fried chicken on his way home from work. We'd fight over the crispy crumbs at the bottom and wash it all down with Coke. On other nights, we ate pizza, marveling at the stretchy cheese and our insatiable appetite for this wondrous food.

A couple of months after my uncle's arrival, he realized that somehow none of the clothes in his suitcase fit him. He had spent the past few weeks wearing his new American wardrobe of T-shirts and sweat suits, clothes that had stretched with his palate. My uncle spent the morning trying on all his old clothes, putting on a fashion show of sorts. With his pants halfway around his bottom, he hopped around telling us that these were the same pants he had worn on the airplane two months ago! Unable to button his shirts, he sucked in his gut and tried not to exhale. My father tried to help him with the various buttons, zippers, and snaps, which refused to button, zip, or snap. It was no use. My uncle had come to America to forget his marital problems. In a way, he had succeeded. Now he had his weight to worry about.

Starting that day, my uncle decided to lose weight. Dragging me along as his interpreter, he and I headed for the Sav-On drugstore to buy diet pills and a scale. We came home feeling hopeful. My uncle swallowed a few pills, then took his regular spot on the sofa to watch the game shows. The next morning, he weighed himself, threw out the diet pills, and dragged me once again to the drugstore. This time, we returned with a powder, which was supposed to be mixed with milk and consumed instead of meals. Since we didn't have a blender, he spent hours in the kitchen, stirring vigorously with a fork, trying to smooth the clumps to make his meals bearable.

A couple of days of this powdered cuisine and my uncle actually lost a few pounds. Things were going well until he decided that adding a couple of scoops of Baskin-Robbins improved the flavor substantially.

Following my uncle's post-diet celebration meal, he discovered that his attempts at dieting had left him with a few souvenir pounds. With renewed dedication, my uncle turned to Plan B. Our marathon television-watching sessions now had a higher purpose. I was to write down the phone numbers for all the products that quickly and painlessly melted away the extra pounds. Ten minutes into *Love, American Style* and we had our catch. I dialed the number on the television screen and ordered the cure. Waiting for the package to arrive, my uncle was on a frenzied mission. Like a soldier making love for the last time before he goes to war, Uncle Nematollah spent the next few days embracing his favorite American foods one last time, some twice. Knowing the end was near, he began trying foods whose siren song we had thus far ignored: Twinkies, tacos, beef jerky, guacamole, and maple syrup.

The package finally arrived. The miracle cure was a stomach girdle. For $19.99, Uncle Nematollah had purchased a scuba-diving outfit of sorts that covered only the stomach, the original owner perhaps having been attacked by a school of sharks. The contraption, when worn for days on end, was supposed to train the wearer to eat less, while firming the stomach muscles. Getting my uncle's overflowing gut to fit the stomach girdle was a task left to my father. Every morning, before going to work, he helped his brother squeeze into his sausage casing, being careful not to trap Nematollah's ample body hair in the zipper. If you ignored the bulging rolls escaping from above and below the stomach girdle, my uncle did look slimmer. But it was hard getting used to his new, erect posture, which prevented him from slumping on the sofa with the rest of us. He strolled around the house admiring his new silhouette, pretending that having his organs crushed was somehow enjoyable. But like all forms of self-inflicted pain, the stomach girdle eventually lost its appeal. It may have been the severe cramping after meals, the inability to slouch, or the welt marks on his skin, but either way, the girdle became history.

Uncle Nematollah's next shortcut to svelteness consisted of a specially constructed exercise outfit, advertised during *The Newlywed Game,* that promised to help sweat away those pesky pounds. The outfit was constructed of a thick silver material, a cross between aluminum foil and vinyl, something perhaps left over from a failed space mission and purchased at a NASA garage sale. The instructions stated that the outfit had to be worn for twenty minutes before each meal, during which the wearer was supposed to engage in some form of exercise. My uncle decided to speed the weight-loss process by wearing his moon suit all day. He thought nothing of circling the block endlessly, leaving neighbors wondering whether perhaps he was looking for the mother ship. Dressed for a jaunt on Venus, he strolled to the supermarket, the hardware store, and everywhere else he needed to go. Unable to understand English, he had apparently forgotten the international meaning of stares as well. Kids at school asked me about the strange guy who was staying with us. In terms of weirdness, my family and I were now off the charts.

The state of euphoria brought on by losing a few pounds soon wore off, accelerated perhaps by the annoying stench of stale sweat emanating from the suit. As far as we knew, the suit was not washable. As attached as he had become to his dehydration chamber, my uncle had to admit it was time to get rid of it.

A few more hours of TV viewing and we placed an order for the Body Shaper. This latest gizmo consisted of a nylon cord attached to several pulleys. By attaching the Body Shaper to a doorknob and lying in the most inconvenient spot possible, the user could exercise one arm or leg, two arms and two legs, one arm and one leg, or any other combination.

Perhaps realizing some contortion fantasy, my uncle was completely hooked on the Body Shaper. He spent his days attached to various doorknobs doing endless leg lifts. Transformed into human scissors, he sliced through the air for hours. We learned the hard way never to open a closed door without first listening for the distinct *swoosh-swoosh* coming from behind the door. It was a mystery why his latest weight-loss gizmo was so successful. We assumed his dedication had something to do with his impending return to Iran and his desire to find a wife. Male peacocks display their feathers to attract the female, but a male human displaying an overflowing gut yields far different results.

A month later, with the Body Shaper having worked its magic, Uncle Nematollah was ready to go home We watched him pack his suitcases, all of us wishing he could stay longer. My uncle had exercised his way into our hearts, and the house was going to seem empty without him.

With a Little Help
from My Friends

I was lucky to have come to America years before the political upheaval in Iran. The Americans we encountered were kind and curious, unafraid to ask questions and willing to listen. As soon as I spoke enough English to communicate, I found myself being interviewed nonstop by children and adults alike. My life became one long-running *Oprah* show, minus the free luxury accommodations in Chicago, and Oprah.

On the topic of Iran, American minds were tabulae rasae. Judging from the questions asked, it was clear that most Americans in 1972 had never heard of Iran. We did our best to educate. "You know Asia? Well, you go south at the Soviet Union and there we are." Or we'd try to be more bucolic, mentioning being south of the beautiful Caspian Sea, "where the famous caviar comes from." Most people in Whittier did not know about the famous caviar and once we explained what it was, they'd scrunch up their faces. "Fish eggs?" they would say. "Gross." We tried mentioning our proximity to Afghanistan or Iraq, but it was no use.

Having exhausted our geographical clues, we would say, "You've heard of India, Japan, or China? We're on the same continent."

We had always known that ours is a small country and that America is very big. But even as a seven-year-old, I was surprised that so many Americans had never noticed us on the map. Perhaps it's like driving a Yugo and realizing that the eighteen-wheeler can't see you.

In Iran, geography is a requirement in every grade. Since the government issues textbooks, every student studies the same material in the same grade. In first-grade geography, I had to learn the shape of Iran and the location of its capital, Tehran. I had to memorize that we shared borders with Turkey, Afghanistan, Pakistan, Iraq, and the USSR. I also knew that I lived on the continent of Asia.

None of the kids in Whittier, a city an hour outside of Los Angeles, ever asked me about geography. They wanted to know about more important things, such as camels. How many did we own back home? What did we feed them? Was it a bumpy ride? I always disappointed them by admitting that I had never seen a camel in my entire life. And as far as a ride goes, our Chevrolet was rather smooth. They reacted as if I had told them that there really was a person in the Mickey Mouse costume.

We were also asked about electricity, tents, and the Sahara. Once again, we disappointed, admitting that we had electricity, that we did not own a tent, and that the Sahara was on another continent. Intent to remedy the image of our homeland as backward, my father took it upon himself to enlighten Americans whenever possible. Any unsuspecting American who asked my father a question received, as a bonus, a lecture on the successful history of the petroleum industry in Iran. As my father droned on, I watched the faces of these kind Americans, who were undoubtedly making mental notes never to talk to a foreigner again.

My family and I wondered why Americans had such a mistaken image of Iran. We were offered a clue one day by a neighbor, who told us that he knew about Iran because he had seen *Lawrence of Arabia*. Whoever Lawrence was, we had never heard of him, we said. My father then explained that Iranians are an Indo-European people; we are not Arabs. We do, however, have two things in common with Saudi Arabia, he continued: "Islam and petroleum." "Now, I won't bore you with religion," he said, "but let me tell you about the petroleum industry."

Another neighbor, a kindly old lady who taught me how to take care of indoor plants, asked whether we had many cats back home. My father, with his uncanny ability to forge friendships, said, "We don't keep pets in our homes. They are dirty." "But your cats are so beautiful!" our neighbor said. We had no idea what she was talking about. Seeing our puzzled expressions, she showed us a picture of a beautiful, longhaired cat. "It's a Persian cat," she said. That was news to us; the only cats we had ever seen back home were the mangy strays that ate scraps behind people's houses. From that day, when I told people I was from Iran, I added "where Persian cats come from." That impressed them.

I tried my best to be a worthy representative of my homeland, but, like a Hollywood celebrity relentlessly pursued by paparazzi, I sometimes got tired of the questions. I, however, never punched anybody with my fists; I used words. One boy at school had a habit of asking me particularly stupid questions. One day he inquired about camels, again. This time, perhaps foreshadowing a vocation in storytelling, I told him that, yes, we had camels, a one-hump and a two-hump. The one-hump belonged to my parents and the two-hump was our family station wagon. His eyes widened.

"Where do you keep them?" he asked.

"In the garage, of course," I told him.

Having heard what he wanted to hear, he ran off to share his knowledge with the rest of the kids on the playground. He was very angry once he realized that I had fooled him, but at least he never asked me another question.

Often kids tried to be funny by chanting, "I ran to I-ran, I ran to I-ran." The correct pronunciation, I always informed them, is "Ee-rahn." "I ran" is a sentence, I told them, as in "I ran away from my geography lesson."

Older boys often asked me to teach them "some bad words in your language." At first, I politely refused. My refusal merely increased their determination, so I solved the problem by teaching them phrases like *man kharam*, which means "I'm an idiot." I told them that what I was teaching them was so nasty that they would have to promise never to repeat it to anyone. They would then spend all of recess running around yelling, "I'm an idiot! I'm an idiot!" I never told them the truth. I figured that someday, somebody would.

But almost every person who asked us a question asked with kindness. Questions were often followed by suggestions of places to visit in California. At school, the same children who inquired about camels also shared their food with me. "I bet you've never tried an Oreo! Have one," or "My mom just baked these peanut butter cookies and she sent you one." Kids invited me to their houses to show me what their rooms looked like. On Halloween, one family brought over a costume, knowing that I would surely be the only kid in the Halloween parade without one. If some-one had been able to encapsulate the kindness of these second-graders in pill form, the pills would undoubtedly put many war correspondents out of business.

After almost two years in Whittier, my father's assignment was completed and we had to return home. The last month of our stay, I attended one slumber party after another, all thrown in my honor. This avalanche of kindness did not make our impending departure any easier. Everyone wanted to know when we would come back to America. We had no answer, but we invited them all to visit us in Iran. I knew no one would ever take us up on our offer, because Iran was off the radar screen for most people. My friends considered visiting their grandmothers in Oregon to be a long trip, so visiting me in Iran was like taking a left turn at the next moon. It wasn't going to happen. I didn't know then that I would indeed be returning to America about two years later.

Between frenzied shopping trips to Sears to buy presents for our relatives back home, my mother spent her last few weeks giving gifts to our American friends. I had wondered why my mother had brought so many Persian handicrafts with her; now I knew. Everyone, from my teachers to the crossing guard to the Brownie leader to the neighbors, received something. "Dees eez from my countay-ree. Es-pay-shay-ley for you," she would explain. These handicrafts, which probably turned up in garage sales the following year, were received with tears and promises to write.

My mother was particularly sad to return to Iran. I had always assumed that she would be relieved to return to her family and to a land where she spoke the language and didn't need me to act as her interpreter. But I realized later that even though my mother could not understand anything the crossing guard, Mrs. Popkin, said, she understood that this woman looked out for me. And she understood her smiles. Even though my mother never attended a Brownie meeting, she knew that the leader, Carrie's mom, opened up her home to us every week and led us through all kinds of projects. No one paid her for this. And my mother knew that when it had been my turn to bring snacks for the class, one of the moms had stepped in and baked cupcakes. My best friend Connie's older sister, Michele, had tried to teach me to ride a bike, and Heather's mom, although single with two daughters, had hosted me overnight more times than I can remember. Even though I had been the beneficiary of all the attention, my mother, watching silently from a distance, had also felt the warmth of generosity and kindness. It was hard to leave.

When my parents and I get together today, we often talk about our first year in America. Even though thirty years have passed, our memories have not faded. We remember the kindness more than ever, knowing that our relatives who immigrated to this country after the Iranian Revolution did not encounter the same America. They saw Americans who had bumper stickers on their cars that read "Iranians: Go Home" or "We Play Cowboys and Iranians." The Americans they met rarely invited them to their houses. These Americans felt that they knew all about Iran and its people, and they had no questions, just opinions. My relatives did not think Americans were very kind.

Bernice

In America, I have an "ethnic" face, a certain immigrant look that says, "I'm not Scandinavian." When I lived in Abadan, my mother and I stood out because we looked foreign. Abadan's desert climate, which resembles that of Palm Springs, produces olive-skinned inhabitants. My mother and I, because of her Turkish ancestry, possess a skin color that on Nicole Kidman is described as "porcelain" and on others as "fish-belly white." In Abadan, people always asked my mother whether she was European. "Well," she'd always gush, "my aunt lives in Germany."

When we moved to California, we no longer looked foreign. With its large Mexican population, Whittier could have passed as our hometown. As long as we didn't open our mouths, we looked as if we belonged. But just one of my mother's signature rambling sentences without a verb ("Shop so good very happy at Sears"), and our cover was blown. Inevitably, people would ask us where we were from, but our answer didn't really matter. One mention of our homeland and people would get that uncomfortable smile on their face that says, "How nice. Where the heck is that?"

In 1976, my father's new job took us to Newport Beach, a coastal town where everyone is blond and sails. There, we stood out like a bunch of Middle Eastern immigrants in a town where everyone is blond and sails. People rarely asked us where we were from, because in Newport Beach, the rule of thumb was "If not blond, then Mexican." People would ask me things like "Could you please tell Lupe that she doesn't have to clean our house next week, since we're going to be on vacation."

One would think that the inhabitants of Newport Beach, a town two hours from the Mexican border, would speak at least a few words of Spanish. But in a place where one's tan is a legitimate topic of conversation ("Is that from last weekend at the beach?" "No, I got this playing tennis yesterday"), learning the language of the domestic help is not a priority.

During my first year in Newport Beach, my junior high was conducting mandatory scoliosis checks. All the sixth-graders were herded into the gym where we waited for the nurses to check the curvature in our backs. When it came my turn, the nurse took a long look at my face and said, "Oh my God! Are you Alaskan?"

"No, I'm Iranian," I replied.

"No way!" she shrieked. "Bernice, doesn't this one look Alaskan?"

As Bernice waddled across the gym, I wanted to make her an offer. "How about I tell Lupe not to come next week since you're going to be on vacation, and we just call it a day?"

During that same year, I was asked to speak about my homeland to a seventh-grade class at my school. The girl who had asked me was a neighbor who needed some extra credit in social studies. I showed up complete with my books in Persian, a doll depicting a villager weaving a Persian rug, several Persian miniatures, and some stuffed grape leaves, courtesy of my mother. I stood in front of the class and said, "Hello, my name is Firoozeh and I'm from Iran." Before I could say anything else, the teacher stood up and said, "Laura, you said she's from Peru!" If my life were a Hollywood musical, this would have been the beginning of the big dance number.

> *You say tomato,*
> *I say tomahto.*
> *You say Persia,*
> *I say Peru.*
> *Let's call the whole thing off.*

So home I went with my Persian miniatures, my doll depicting a villager weaving a Persian rug, and my books. At least my mother didn't have to cook dinner that night, since the thirty grape leaves were enough for all of us.

During our stay in Newport Beach, the Iranian Revolution took place and a group of Americans were taken hostage in the American embassy in Tehran. Overnight, Iranians living in America became, to say the least, very unpopular. For some reason, many Americans began to think that all Iranians, despite outward appearances to the contrary, could at any given moment get angry and take prisoners. People always asked us what we thought of the hostage situation. "It's awful," we always said. This reply was generally met with surprise. We were asked our opinion on the hostages so often that I started reminding people that they weren't in our garage. My mother solved the problem by claiming to be from Russia or "Torekey." Sometimes I'd just say, "Have you noticed how all the recent serial killers have been Americans? I won't hold it against you."

From Newport Beach, I moved to Berkeley, a town once described as the armpit of California. But Berkeley wasn't just any armpit, it was an armpit in need of a shave and a shower, an armpit full of well-read people who had not only heard of Iran but knew something about it. In Berkeley, people were either thrilled or horrified to meet an Iranian. Reactions included "So what do you think of the fascist American CIA pigs who supported the Shah's dictatorship only to use him as a puppet in their endless thirst for power in the Middle East and other areas like Nicaragua?" Sometimes, mentioning that I was from Iran completely ended the conversation. I never knew why, but I assume some feared that I might really be yet another female terrorist masquerading as a history of art major at UC–Berkeley. My favorite category of question, however, assumed that all Iranians were really just one big family: "Do you know Ali Akbari in Cincinnati?" people would ask. "He's so nice."

During my years at Berkeley, I met François, a Frenchman who later became my husband. It was during our friendship that I realized how unfair my life had truly been. Being French in America is like having your hand stamped with one of those passes that allows you to get into everything. All François has to do is mention his obviously French name and people find him intriguing. It is assumed that he's a sensitive, well-read intellectual, someone who, when not reciting Baudelaire, spends his days creating Impressionist paintings.

Every American seems to have a favorite France story. "It was the loveliest café and I can still taste the *tarte tatin*!" As far as I know, François had not made that *tarte tatin*, although people are more than happy to give him credit. "You know," I always add,

"France has an ugly colonial past." But it doesn't matter. People see my husband and think of Gene Kelly dancing with Leslie Caron. People see me and think of hostages.

This is why, in my next life, I am applying to come back as a Swede. I assume that as a Swede, I will be a leggy blonde. Should God get things confused and send me back as a Swede trapped in the body of a Middle Eastern woman, I'll just pretend I'm French.

A Dozen Key Chains

In my large extended family, each member has a reputation. This reputation, carved in stone, is usually the result of a somewhat random act that for some unknown reason takes on a far greater meaning, and becomes the defining moment in a life. At the tender age of five, for instance, my cousin Ardesheer developed the nasty habit of defecating behind his parents' living room curtains during their frequent formal dinner parties. Today someone might interpret this behavior as a sign of anger, since the poor tot was stuck with a nanny against his wishes while the other family members reveled. Instead, it came to serve as a reflection of the type of person he really is. Having outgrown his annoying and unique routine, Ardesheer went on to become a restaurant owner. Recently at a family gathering that took place during a slow patch in his otherwise successful career, someone mentioned that Ardesheer's restaurant wasn't doing too well. To this my aunt replied, "Well, what do you expect from someone who poops behind curtains?"

As much as Ardesheer has suffered from his reputation, my older brother Farshid continues to thrive on his. When Farshid was in kindergarten back in Abadan, he was, according to all reports, an extremely popular and charismatic little person. This may not seem like such a big deal in other families, but my parents, both of whom are painfully shy, looked upon their outgoing anomaly just as Native Americans regard an albino buffalo—he was a miracle. Forty years after completing kindergarten, my brother is still consulted before all decisions big or small. Farshid has steered endless numbers of cousins and second cousins through decisions ranging from which type of car to buy to which courses to take in college to which nasal decongestant works best. Nobody is more devoted to Farshid's decision-making prowess than my parents, and Farshid, like James Bond, has never turned down an assignment.

When I was eleven years old, I told my parents I wanted to go to camp. The year was 1976, and I had lived in America for a total of two years. Except for some sleepovers back in second grade, I had never spent the night away from my parents. I cannot remember what possessed me to want to try summer camp. I'm not sure I even knew what one did at camp. But for whatever reason, I made the announcement, and my parents immediately assigned Farshid, who was then eighteen, the task of finding the right camp for me.

After much research, Farshid found the "perfect" camp: Pine Lodge Mountain Summer Camp, located in the Mammoth Mountains, a mere eight-hour drive from my house. My father, whose cultlike devotion to Farshid rules out the possibility of questioning any of Farshid's decisions, was very impressed that the camp cost $500 for two weeks. Anything that expensive has to be good, he repeatedly said. The Pine Lodge brochure also came with a stamp of approval from a camp organization that none of us had ever heard of, but which further impressed my father. My mother, as usual, had no comment, although twenty years later, she did say, "I didn't think you should've gone."

After signing up for Pine Lodge Mountain Summer Camp, I received a list of supplies I would need, none of which we owned. The following Saturday, my father and I set out for Montgomery Ward. My father, whose aversion to shopping is well known, believes anything that costs more than it did back in Ahwaz in 1946 is overpriced. Fortunately, he is always willing to pay for classes and experiences that promote growth of some sort. But everything else is too expensive. His inability to pay full price for anything explains why he owns what is, as far as we know, the only maroon-and-pink suede pair of Nikes in existence. The items he has picked up on clearance tables range from merely useless, like his portable siren, to truly atrocious, like birds made of felt. And even he has admitted that people do stare at his maroon Nikes in a way that suggests something other than envy. But the magnetic pull of a bargain is simply too strong.

List in hand, my father and I headed straight for the clearance section in the camping department. The first item on our list was a sleeping bag. Unfortunately for me, there happened to be one on sale. Although I knew nothing about sleeping bags, I did notice that this one was considerably larger and bulkier than the ones not on sale. While the others rolled up and fit neatly into small drawstring bags, this one was the size of our kitchen table, which my father had bought at an auction of seized goods. I did point out to my father that this particular sleeping bag did not come with a drawstring bag. My father assured me that he would find some kind of bag at home. After all, you'd have to be stupid to pass up a sleeping bag that cost only $8.99!

We continued down the list and purchased the cheapest version of everything, skipping the "optional" items entirely. Those, my father explained, were for people who just liked to buy stuff. Inflatable mattress, wide-brimmed hat, insect repellent—who needed all that extra baggage?

We brought home our purchases and proceeded to examine each object as if it were a meteor that had landed in our living room. A mesh bag for laundry! Stackable tin plates that converted to frying pans! An aluminum canteen with a built-in cup! These purchases, coupled with the picture of the smiling girl riding a horse on the camp brochure, left little doubt in my mind that Pine Lodge Mountain Summer Camp meant nonstop fun and adventure.

The only doubt lingering in my mind concerned the sleeping bag. Despite my father's reassurance, there existed no bag in our house big enough to hold this monstrosity. No matter how much my brother, father, and I sat on the sleeping bag, we could not make it any less bulky. It defied flattening. The synthetic material used to stuff my sleeping bag would have been much better utilized in some other place, like freeway dividers, but for now I was stuck with the King Kong of all sleeping bags and nothing to put it in. Finally, my father, with his "mind of an engineer," came up with a brilliant solution: a Hefty trash bag.

A few months later, my father and I drove to the bus stop together. Like any other child going to overnight camp for the first time, I immediately regretted my decision. My father did his best to calm me by telling me stories of his first year in America as a Fulbright scholar at Texas A&M. He spoke fondly of his Pakistani roommate, who made delicious curry, but whose name he no longer remembered. My father's stories made one fact abundantly clear: I did not want to go to camp.

We arrived at the bus stop only to discover that all the other kids had signed up with at least one friend. My family had just moved from Whittier to Newport Beach, so I didn't have a friend anywhere, especially at this bus stop. To make matters worse, everyone was staring at my Hefty trash bag.

We finally boarded the bus. I sat by myself and secretly wished that some kind person would sit next to me and be my friend. No one sat next to me. As the bus ride began, I was acutely aware of how much fun all the kids around me seemed to be having. Giggles and laughter filled the bus. After a few hours on the road, the boy behind me tapped me on the shoulder.

"Hey, can I ask you a question?" he said.

"Sure!" I answered.

"Well," he said, "do you look down a lot?"

"No, why?" I asked.

"Well, your nose points downward so I figured that's because you're always looking at the ground or something."

Upon hearing this, all the kids around me burst out laughing.

Hours later, we arrived at camp. Pine Lodge was a converted two-story house. All the boys stayed downstairs and all the girls stayed on the second floor. In the girls' room stood rows of bunk beds. There was one bathroom on the floor for all the girls to share. Oddly, the door to the bathroom had been removed, so any girl who needed to use the toilet or the sink could walk in on someone taking a shower. Coming from a modest culture and an even more modest family, I had never seen another person naked, not even my mother, so the idea that someone could walk into the bathroom while I was naked in the shower seemed unbelievable. I decided then and there not to bathe.

Out of the eleven other girls in my room, ten appeared to be mean. Mary, who slept on the top of my bunk, was the only girl who would speak to me, or rather cry to me. I liked her right away, not as a friend, but as someone who made me look good.

Mary and her younger brother, Willy, were both campers, and they spent all day trying to be on the same team for all activities and all night crying at the idea of being separated. I had never known a brother and sister who actually enjoyed each other's company so much. I soon discovered it wasn't that they enjoyed each other's company so much as they were simply afraid of everybody else. The two of them managed to be the butt of every joke. Mary felt responsible for Willy, whose Coke-bottle glasses and tendency to tremble made him an easy target for all the boys. Mary, herself, was not much more resilient. All someone had to do to reduce her to tears was to call her a name, any name. Mary and Willy were a huge source of comfort to me, not only because they hated Pine Lodge Mountain Summer Camp as much as I did but because they were the ones whom everyone picked on. I knew that in the pecking order of favorite targets for mean kids, I followed Mary and her brother. But those two, between their crying, their trembling, and their throwing up when nervous, proved far more satisfying targets than I could ever have hoped to be. In fact, not only did I not get picked on, but I was completely ignored by everyone, including the counselors. Had it not been for Mary's sobbing to me every night, I could have sworn I was at a Zen retreat.

Since I wasn't going to bathe, I decided to minimize getting dirty by participating only in arts and crafts. I skipped the horseback riding, the overnight campout, the archery lessons, the hikes to the Indian grounds, and basically every activity outlined in the camp brochure. Every morning I showed up at the macramé station ready to make another key chain.

At the end of the first week, the counselors announced that the camp would be putting on a play called *Fiddler on the Roof* and everyone would have to participate. Each camper was assigned a role. I was to play the ghost of the grandmother. Even though I had only one line, the role required that I be covered head to toe with talcum powder. I now suspect that this was a ploy to encourage me to bathe.

The night of the play, one of the counselors started to apply the talcum powder but soon ran into a problem. A week's worth of oil had accumulated on my hair and body, and the talcum powder clumped the instant it touched me. Rather than look like a ghost, I resembled someone who'd been dunked in a vat of bread dough.

After the play, I really wanted to bathe, but I simply could not. The idea of any of the mean girls walking in on me as I took a shower was just too much. Plus, I had achieved such a near-invisible status, I didn't think anyone would notice how dirty I was. Nobody, except for the macramé teacher, Pat, ever talked to me, so I had no motivation to risk humiliation in exchange for hygiene.

Finally, the last day of camp arrived. I put on the one clean T-shirt I had saved for this day, packed my twelve key chains, rolled the sleeping bag into its trash bag, and waited for the bus. I didn't have to worry about any emotional good-byes since this was, by far, my happiest day at camp. I exchanged addresses only with Pat. I didn't have much to say to Mary, since our relationship was based entirely on her sobbing and my listening. I wondered whether her father would be angry if he'd learned he had spent $1,000 on camp for his kids and they had done nothing but cry. I, at least, had my key chains, and by the second week, even Pat had remarked on the quality of my knots.

I arrived at the bus station to find my father and oldest brother, Farid, waiting for me. Upon seeing me, Farid screamed, "You stink! Didn't you bathe at all?" All of a sudden, I realized the gravity of the situation. I had not washed my body in two weeks. Having lost my near-invisible camp status, I was overcome with embarrassment and shame. "Of course I bathed!" I replied.

During the car ride back, my father asked me if I had enjoyed camp. "It was great!" I said. I knew he had sent me to camp expecting $500 worth of fun, and I didn't have the heart to tell him the truth. So instead of weaving key chains, I spent the next few weeks weaving stories of all my great adventures. I don't know whether my father believed me, but at least I earned a reputation as the best key-chain maker in the family.

You Can Call Me Al

My father's favorite spot on Planet Earth is Las Vegas. As a child, I had to endure endless "vacations" to that den o' sin in the desert. Whenever a three- or four-day weekend rolled around, my father would happily announce, "We're going to Las Vegas!" I hated it, but Las Vegas was cheap and so was my father, so off we went.

Las Vegas was a four-hour drive from our house. The highway leading to this Promised Land cut through the desert, which meant that watching the scenery from the backseat of our Chevrolet rivaled the thrill of watching a fishing show. My brothers, both of them in college, were spared these trips. I envied them.

The ritual was always the same. We would have to wake up by 5:00 A.M. so we could be on the road by 5:15. The day before our trip, the gas tank was filled, the engine checked, the suitcases packed, and the windshield cleaned, all courtesy of my father. The most important part of our ritual involved my mother's holding the Koran at the top of the doorframe while we each walked under it. For my parents, this ensured a safe journey—

they hoped one without speeding tickets. I always found it unsettling to invoke religion in anything having to do with Las Vegas, a place that I'm quite sure the Prophet Muhammad would not have approved of.

We always drove for one hour before stopping for breakfast at Denny's. My father's devotion to Denny's restaurants approached religious fervor. To him, Denny's was a clean oasis where the waitresses were always friendly. We didn't really like the food, but that seemed a small price to pay for a clean bathroom in the middle of the desert. After breakfast, we'd get back in the car, turn on the air conditioner, and keep driving. We didn't stop until the next Denny's, where we'd have a snack and my father would say how amazing it was that all Denny's could be so clean, no matter where they were. "America is a great country," he'd always add.

Once we reached Las Vegas, we always went to the Stardust. There, my father would go to the front desk and ask for his special friend, a man who had asked to be called Al. Despite the "No Vacancy" sign, the mighty Al would get us a room. This clandestine operation, however, required a handshake with a five-dollar bill enclosed. My father loved his Frank Sinatra moment and always told stories about the exchanges between him and Al, stretching a five-minute encounter into a two-hour story. I hated Al and always hoped he'd end up in jail, but he, like the decks of cards adorned with pictures of naked women, was a fixture at the Stardust. Years later, I asked my father why he never made room reservations in advance. "That would have been too boring," he said.

Once we settled into our room, my father headed straight for the blackjack tables. Everyone except gamblers knows that gambling never pays. My father always believed that he was *this close* to the big one, but because of some unforeseen event, like someone else winning, he'd lost. Losing, like winning, only increased his determination to play. At the blackjack table, my father became strangely superstitious, blaming his losses on seemingly unrelated events. He never sat at a table where anyone wore a hat, since that was bad luck. Redheads were good luck, but only if they were women. Redheaded men were bad luck. People who talked too much were bad luck, as were people who were strangely silent. My favorite of his wacky beliefs was that non-Americans at the table were bad luck. I couldn't resist suggesting that maybe he should stay home since, as a foreigner, he was his own biggest source of bad luck. My father never appreciated that observation.

A few hours after our arrival, my mother would declare that it was time to go find my father. Minors were not allowed in the gambling area, so like moons orbiting the earth, we circled the perimeter of the casino, looking for my father's signature receding hairline. During our many revolutions, we noticed a correlation between receding hairlines and blackjack, as well as a relationship between outdated bouffant hairdos and slot machines.

Once we'd spotted him, I'd wait near the main entrance while my mother went to fetch him. My father considered the sight of my mother approaching him to be a certain sign of bad luck.

It was then time for the $3.99 all-you-can-eat buffet, during which we unfortunately had to listen to my father's gambling stories. These didn't change much from trip to trip and involved a lot of "almosts." I hated these stories as much as I hated Al, because I had figured out that nobody leaves Las Vegas a winner.

The all-you-can-eat buffet, that American phenomenon, represented the only endurance exercise at which my family excelled. Even when my father had just lost hundreds of dollars at the blackjack table, we felt that we were beating the system by filling ourselves with more food than we were actually paying for. "These shrimp alone are worth at least five dollars!" my father would declare. "Look at those desserts! They're worth the price of the buffet by themselves!" my mom and I would chime in. By stuffing ourselves until we ached, we felt we had outsmarted Las Vegas. And all for only $3.99!

What made Las Vegas even more awful were my memories of real vacations we had taken in the past. In Iran, "vacation" meant going to the Caspian Sea. Every summer, my father's employer, the National Iranian Oil Company, allowed its employees the use of its villas in Mahmood Abad for one week. Mahmood Abad, a town on the Caspian shore, was a two-day drive from Abadan. Every summer, the five of us would pile into our Chevrolet, my mom making sure to bring enough sandwiches, cucumbers, fruit, and Coca-Cola for the long drive. We were always glad to leave Abadan in the summer, since its desert climate was unbearable. As we headed north, toward Tehran, the weather cooled off slowly, proof that we were indeed farther and farther from our home. We always reached Tehran in the evening and spent the night at relatives' houses. The next morning, we set off again, complete with fresh sandwiches and fruit courtesy of my relatives.

The drive between Tehran and the Caspian Sea is one of the most beautiful stretches of land I have ever seen. The lush scenery offered more shades of green than I saw anywhere else. We passed by endless fields of purple wildflowers. The most exciting part of the trip was the many tunnels, which enabled us to pass through the Elburz Mountains to reach the Caspian. We knew we were almost there by the change in the climate: the closer we came, the fresher and crisper the air. The sight of villagers hawking cheap plastic pails, beach balls, and shell neck-laces along the road meant one thing: we were almost at the sea. We could no longer contain our excitement.

The "villas" we stayed in were modest cabins lined up along the beach like dominoes. Days were spent at the beach, where we built sand castles, looked for seashells, and played in the waves. Knowing the children were safely occupied, my parents relaxed and mingled with friends. Meals were eaten in the mess hall, cafeteria style. At night, everyone returned to the cafeteria for the nightly movie. In retrospect, our vacation was like a fam-ily camp and everyone was sad to leave. "How can a week go by so quickly?" we'd always ask.

In America, we lived on the California coast but rarely went to the beach. The water was too cold and the waves too big. Longing for warm water one year, we decided to vacation in Hawaii. My father booked a one-week stay in Waikiki. "We're staying right on the beach!" he announced. Having never been to Hawaii, I expected a relaxing tropical paradise, somewhere like Gilligan's Island.

We arrived in Waikiki to discover that an "ocean view" room meant we had to stand on our balcony and crane our necks to catch a speck of blue in the far corner. In between the high-rises sat shops declaring "I Got Lei-d in Hawaii!" on T-shirts, mugs, and towels. Everywhere I went, I saw the same carved coconuts, the same seashell frames, and the same hats, all made in the Philippines. I tried to hang loose, but Waikiki felt more like 7-Eleven-by-the-Sea.

The following year, we decided to vacation on Kauai, an is-land in Hawaii that the travel agent described as a true tropical paradise. The description was accurate. Our one-story hotel sat in the middle of a lush forest. On our first day, we experienced quick tropical rains followed by spectacular rainbows. Vibrant flowers, so big and rich in color that they almost looked fake, dotted the plants around our hotel. We had found God's hide-away.

On our second day, my parents announced that Kauai was boring. "There's nothing to look at, just plants and rainbows," my father declared. "There are no stores," added my mother. Instead of staying for another week, we left the next day.

The following year, my father decided to take us to Yosemite National Park for a week. Uncle Nematollah was staying with us then. My father booked two cabins and off we went for another taste of paradise. Eight hours later, we arrived in the beautiful Yosemite Valley. We oohed and aahed at the spectacular scenery. The first day, we explored the surrounding area, wading in a nearby stream. All was perfect until my uncle, who didn't speak English but who could nonetheless identify a picture of a bear's head with a line through it, asked my father to translate the signs posted near our cabin. My father explained that the signs warned campers of bears that often came looking for food. Upon hearing this, my mother and uncle decided we had to leave Yosemite right away. My mother was convinced that the bears were lined up in the nearby bushes waiting for their chance at the all-you-can-eat Persian buffet. "We can't leave!" I protested. "We just got here!" My mother was already packing the suitcases. I tried my best to reason with her. "The signs say that the bears are attracted by the smell of food, not people."

An hour later, we were in the car, headed for the bear-free suburbs.

After that trip, my father declared that, with the sole exception of Las Vegas, his favorite vacation spot was "right here on the sofa in front of the television set." My mother declared that my father was a bore. And I decided that as soon as I was grown up, I would travel the world looking for rainbows and bears. But before that, I'd have to see Al one more time so I could suggest a great vacation spot for him. "Just keep plenty of food on you at all times," I'd tell him, "especially when you sleep!"

Of Mosquitoes and Men

My husband, François, loves to travel. When I first met him, he regaled me with stories of exotic places he had visited: the Maldive Islands, West Africa, Bali, Sri Lanka. He told me stories about his Greek grandfather, Savas, who traveled to Baghdad to set up the city's first leavened-bread factory. A few months after his arrival, he suffered a minor cut during his daily shave. The seemingly innocuous cut became infected. Penicillin had not yet reached Baghdad, and Savas died a few days later, leaving behind a wife and two young daughters. In keeping with local tradition, Savas was buried in a Muslim ceremony. A few nights later, François's Belgian grandmother, Octavie, went to the gravesite at midnight with two young men, a Roman Catholic priest, and a shovel. She had her husband dug up, then reburied in a Catholic ceremony.

Before Baghdad, Savas and Octavie had lived in the Congo, where Octavie had a beloved baby buffalo. This gentle creature hung around their home like a family pet. But, like all buffalo, he eventually grew big and turned into the proverbial bull in the china shop. Having been domesticated, he could no longer be returned to the wild, so Octavie decided to send him to the zoo in Antwerp. After a teary good-bye, she placed the buffalo on a steamship bound for Belgium. But, alas, the zoo never received its newest addition. Somewhere between the Congo and Belgium, the cook had developed a hankering for buffalo stew.

François also told me that when he first attended kindergarten in Paris, his teacher called his parents after a week to inform them that their son was exhibiting inappropriate behavior and needed to see a psychologist immediately. Apparently, François was unable to keep his clothes on at school. His mother had to explain that, having spent his formative years in Africa, he wasn't used to wearing clothes. Given time, she said, he would surely adjust.

I loved all of François's stories and never had to impress him with any exotic tales, since as far as he was concerned, being Iranian and having a name like Firoozeh far outweighed any of his adventures. I didn't quite agree with him, but who was I to burst the bubble of a man whom I had somehow managed to effortlessly impress, a man who was captivated by the mere details of my life? Every so often, I would toss out some piddly story about the caviar vendors beside the Caspian Sea or the smell of nasturtiums in my aunt Sedigeh's garden, and the Frenchman went gaga. By the time I told him about the frog infestation in Ahwaz, he wanted to marry me.

All was well until we started to plan our honeymoon. François had told me that he wanted to take me to "the most romantic place on earth." That sounded good. "We're going to go to a former palace," he had continued. Was this really my life, or had I, through some wrinkle in time, stepped into somebody else's universe, like maybe Grace Kelly's? But like every good fantasy, this one lasted about thirty seconds. That's when François told me that this romantic getaway was in India. I tried to conceal my shock, but for me, "India" and "honeymoon" just didn't belong in the same sentence. As much as I love Indian music, literature, and food, I had never felt the need to go there on my honeymoon. I feel about India the way I feel while watching those Jacques Cousteau adventures where the divers explore undersea caves, flashing their lights in the pitch-black crevices only to discover that the cave is teeming with sharks and giant squid. Yes, it's breathtaking, but from my sofa. Do I want to don a wet suit and join Jacques in those frigid waters? *Non, merci.*

François was very disappointed that several weeks of planning had been met with "Are you kidding?" I tried to explain to him that for me, a vacation does not involve certain hardships including, but not limited to, mosquitoes, vaccinations, poor plumbing, or stomach ailments. Having grown up in southern Iran, I experienced enough physical discomforts to make me truly appreciate a nice resort. François's life of affluence in the Parisian suburbs, on the other hand, had left him itching for adventure. The only itching I felt was caused by the constant mosquito bites I got in Abadan. To François's family, a vacation meant going to their secluded seaside villa in Greece, where they brushed up on their tanning and windsurfing skills. These activities were interspersed with fishing or looking for ancient relics that washed up on the beach. To my family, a vacation usually meant going to a relative's house and sleeping on the floor, squeezed between several cousins. François enjoyed traveling throughout Greece on rickety buses—such a refreshing contrast to the orderly and predictable Parisian Métro. I had to ride a similar bus to school in fourth grade, and I found it neither quaint nor charming. Ignoring any notions of safety, the bus driver packed in twice as many kids as seats. Since I was one of the last to be picked up, I had to stand in the aisle, squeezed between the other kids like an egg in a tightly packed tin of beluga caviar. One day, the girl behind me threw up all over me on the way to school. The driver kept driving. By the time I reached school, I was in tears, but the teacher would not let me go home. I had to spend the entire day with dried vomit all over my uniform while all the kids around me held their noses.

During other vacations, François saw the sights in Thailand and Bali. The only sights we ever chose to see were the faces of family members who lived in other towns. François's family thought large bugs and humidity were exotic; we worshiped the guys who invented climate control and bug spray. We never sought exotic forms of discomfort; they were part of a package deal that came with our homeland.

I remember being five years old and going to the bazaar in Abadan with my mother and needing desperately to go to the bathroom. The only bathrooms available were "Turkish" ones, which consist of a hole in the ground. If odor could be measured in decibels, these toilets were the equivalent of front-row seats at a heavy metal concert. Needless to say, I just couldn't get myself to use any of them. Besides setting a bladder endurance record, I learned never to drink anything on the morning of bazaar day.

As much as I loved living in Abadan, I hated the heat and the mosquitoes. If everyone has a lifetime quota of bug bites, I reached mine by age six. My father used to tell me that I must be the sweetest person because the mosquitoes bit me more than anyone else. The constant itching combined with the oppressive heat made me truly appreciate modern touches like powerful air conditioners and screen doors. When we came to California, one of the first things I noticed was the pleasant absence of mosquitoes.

After almost two delightful mosquito-free years in Whittier, we returned to Iran. My mother and I went to live in Ahwaz with my aunt Fatimeh, while my father worked in Tehran. Ahwaz, in southern Iran, is a town generously endowed with dirt and dust. Everything that moved on the unpaved streets, whether people, donkeys, or cars, only served to relocate the dirt from the ground to the face of anyone who happened to be walking down the same path. It rarely rained, but when it did, the dirt became mud, and mud on the face is far more annoying than dirt.

I was slow to adjust to my new, more physically challenging surroundings. Just when I was getting used to the taste of dust in my mouth, along came a frog infestation of biblical proportions. Tiny frogs covered the town. The streets undulated under a blanket of frogs. Before we entered any building, we had to scrape off the layer of sticky frog guts clinging to our shoes. No matter how quickly we opened and closed the front door of our house, five or six frogs managed to hop in. We always found the intruders eventually, but in the most unlikely places. I never quite got used to hearing my mother scream, "How did the frog get in *there?*" This went on for a couple of weeks, until the frogs mysteriously disappeared and frog innards were, thankfully, no longer a part of my daily life.

The next time I saw frogs close up, I was on my honeymoon in Paris. François and I were staying in a beautiful hotel with great plumbing and no mosquitoes. This time, the frogs were not covering the bottom of my shoe but instead were covered with a light *persillade* and came with a side of asparagus. They were *much* better that way.

The "F Word"

My cousin's name, Farbod, means "Greatness." When he moved to America, all the kids called him "Farthead." My brother Farshid ("He Who Enlightens") became "Fartshit." The name of my friend Neggar means "Beloved," although it can be more accurately translated as "She Whose Name Almost Incites Riots." Her brother Arash ("Giver") initially couldn't understand why every time he'd say his name, people would laugh and ask him if it itched.

All of us immigrants knew that moving to America would be fraught with challenges, but none of us thought that our names would be such an obstacle. How could our parents have ever imagined that someday we would end up in a country where monosyllabic names reign supreme, a land where "William" is shortened to "Bill," where "Susan" becomes "Sue," and "Richard" somehow evolves into "Dick"? America is a great country, but nobody without a mask and a cape has a *z* in his name. And have Americans ever realized the great scope of the guttural sounds they're missing? Okay, so it has to do with linguistic roots, but I do believe this would be a richer country if all Americans could do a little tongue aerobics and learn to pronounce "kh," a sound more commonly associated in this culture with phlegm, or "gh," the sound usually made by actors in the final moments of a choking scene. It's like adding a few new spices to the kitchen pantry. Move over, cinnamon and nutmeg, make way for cardamom and sumac.

Exotic analogies aside, having a foreign name in this land of Joes and Marys is a pain in the spice cabinet. When I was twelve, I decided to simplify my life by adding an American middle name. This decision serves as proof that sometimes simplifying one's life in the short run only complicates it in the long run.

My name, Firoozeh, chosen by my mother, means "Turquoise" in Persian. In America, it means "Unpronounceable" or "I'm Not Going to Talk to You Because I Cannot Possibly Learn Your Name and I Just Don't Want to Have to Ask You Again and Again Because You'll Think I'm Dumb or You Might Get Upset or Something." My father, incidentally, had wanted to name me Sara. I do wish he had won that argument.

To strengthen my decision to add an American name, I had just finished fifth grade in Whittier, where all the kids incessantly called me "Ferocious." That summer, my family moved to Newport Beach, where I looked forward to starting a new life. I wanted to be a kid with a name that didn't draw so much attention, a name that didn't come with a built-in inquisition as to when and why I had moved to America and how was it that I spoke English without an accent and was I planning on going back and what did I think of America?

My last name didn't help any. I can't mention my maiden name, because:

"Dad, I'm writing a memoir."

"Great! Just don't mention our name."

Suffice it to say that, with eight letters, including a *z*, and four syllables, my last name is as difficult and foreign as my first. My first and last name together generally served the same purpose as a high brick wall. There was one exception to this rule. In Berkeley, and only in Berkeley, my name drew people like flies to baklava. These were usually people named Amaryllis or Chrysanthemum, types who vacationed in Costa Rica and to whom lentils described a type of burger. These folks were probably not the pride of Poughkeepsie, but they were refreshingly nonjudgmental.

When I announced to my family that I wanted to add an American name, they reacted with their usual laughter. Never one to let mockery or good judgment stand in my way, I proceeded to ask for suggestions. My father suggested "Fifi." Had I had a special affinity for French poodles or been considering a career in prostitution, I would've gone with that one. My mom suggested "Farah," a name easier than "Firoozeh" yet still Iranian. Her reasoning made sense, except that Farrah Fawcett was at the height of her popularity and I didn't want to be associated with somebody whose poster hung in every postpubescent boy's bedroom. We couldn't think of any American names beginning with *F*, so we moved on to *J*, the first letter of our last name. I don't know why we limited ourselves to names beginning with my initials, but it made sense at that moment, perhaps by the logic employed moments before bungee jumping. I finally chose the name "Julie" mainly for its simplicity. My brothers, Farid and Farshid, thought that adding an American name was totally stupid. They later became Fred and Sean.

That same afternoon, our doorbell rang. It was our new next-door neighbor, a friendly girl my age named Julie. She asked me my name and after a moment of hesitation, I introduced myself as Julie. "What a coincidence!" she said. I didn't mention that I had been Julie for only half an hour.

Thus I started sixth grade with my new, easy name and life became infinitely simpler. People actually remembered my name, which was an entirely refreshing new sensation. All was well until the Iranian Revolution, when I found myself with a new set of problems. Because I spoke English without an accent and was known as Julie, people assumed I was American. This meant that I was often privy to their real feelings about those "damn I-raynians." It was like having those X-ray glasses that let you see people naked, except that what I was seeing was far uglier than people's underwear. It dawned on me that these people would have probably never invited me to their house had they known me as Firoozeh. I felt like a fake.

When I went to college, I eventually went back to using my real name. All was well until I graduated and started looking for a job. Even though I had graduated with honors from UC–Berkeley, I couldn't get a single interview. I was guilty of being a humanities major, but I began to suspect that there was more to my problems. After three months of rejections, I added "Julie" to my résumé. Call it coincidence, but the job offers started coming in. Perhaps it's the same kind of coincidence that keeps African Americans from getting cabs in New York.

Once I got married, my name became Julie Dumas. I went from having an identifiably "ethnic" name to having ancestors who wore clogs. My family and non-American friends continued calling me Firoozeh, while my coworkers and American friends called me Julie. My life became one big knot, especially when friends who knew me as Julie met friends who knew me as Firoozeh. I felt like those characters in soap operas who have an evil twin. The two, of course, can never be in the same room, since they're played by the same person, a struggling actress who wears a wig to play one of the twins and dreams of moving on to bigger and better roles. I couldn't blame my mess on a screen-writer; it was my own doing.

I decided to untangle the knot once and for all by going back to my real name. By then, I was a stay-at-home mom, so I really didn't care whether people remembered my name or gave me job interviews. Besides, most of the people I dealt with were in dia-pers and were in no position to judge. I was also living in Silicon Valley, an area filled with people named Rajeev, Avishai, and Insook.

Every once in a while, though, somebody comes up with a new permutation and I am once again reminded that I am an immigrant with a foreign name. I recently went to have blood drawn for a physical exam. The waiting room for blood work at our local medical clinic is in the basement of the building, and no matter how early one arrives for an appointment, forty coughing, wheezing people have gotten there first. Apart from reading *Golf Digest* and *Popular Mechanics*, there isn't much to do except guess the number of contagious diseases represented in the windowless room. Every ten minutes, a name is called and everyone looks to see which cough matches that name. As I waited patiently, the receptionist called out, "Fritzy, Fritzy!" Everyone looked around, but no one stood up. Usually, if I'm waiting to be called by some-one who doesn't know me, I will respond to just about any name starting with an *F*. Having been called Froozy, Frizzy, Fiorucci, and Frooz and just plain "Uhhhh . . . ," I am highly accommo-dating. I did not, however, respond to "Fritzy" because there is, as far as I know, no *t* in my name. The receptionist tried again, "Fritzy, Fritzy DumbAss." As I stood up to this most linguistically original version of my name, I could feel all eyes upon me. The room was momentarily silent as all of these sick people sat united in a moment of gratitude for their own names.

Despite a few exceptions, I have found that Americans are now far more willing to learn new names, just as they're far more willing to try new ethnic foods. Of course, some people just don't like to learn. One mom at my children's school adamantly refused to learn my "impossible" name and instead settled on calling me "F Word." She was recently transferred to New York where, from what I've heard, she might meet an immigrant or two and, who knows, she just might have to make some room in her spice cabinet.

Waterloo

My father is a proud man. He was the first member of his family to study in America, the first to win a Fulbright scholarship, and, years later, the first to settle permanently in America. Because of him, his siblings and their families ended up in Southern California, where they all live within half an hour of one another. "I am the Christopher Columbus of the family," he always says.

Nothing, however, has made my father as proud as his role as the family swim instructor. In Iran, people learned to swim on their own, if they learned at all. My mother, like most women of her generation, never learned to swim. Neither did four of her five sisters, or her brother. This was the norm. My father, always the progressive man, decided that every one of his children and his nieces and nephews would learn to swim. Abadan, having been built by the British, contained many luxuries not readily found in other areas, including a clubhouse with a large pool. Every summer my relatives came from all over Iran to stay with us, and, sure enough, it was always some child's turn to learn to swim. Like a game-show host announcing the next contestant, my father would say, "This summer, it's *your* turn, Mahmood!"

My father had a perfect track record, a topic he loved to talk about. "I have a gift," he'd always say. We had all resigned ourselves to having to listen over and over again to his description of the exact moment at which each niece and nephew learned to swim and the spellbinding tension leading up to it. "Mahmood said, 'Uncle Kazem, I can't do this,' and I said, 'Yes, you can,' and he lifted his arm like this and I pushed him a little bit and he kicked like this and he started to swim like a fish, so I said, 'Hey, you never told me you knew how to swim!' " He'd always end these riveting tales by telling us, "You should've been there!" We were all glad we hadn't been. The stories were interesting the first fourteen times, but beyond that, they became the equivalent of the neighbor's vacation slides showing the cathedrals of France from all angles. Unfortunately, there just wasn't much anyone could do to put an end to these tales. Each new swimmer represented a victory, and talking about it made my father relive his moments of glory over and over again. The twinkle in his eye, the excitement in his voice, the pride in his face all made it clear that my father would never stop retelling his stories.

History, however, has shown us that even the greatest of generals must eventually face defeat in battle, and thus was carved my destiny. I was my father's Waterloo.

My father, an engineer, had an entirely logical approach to teaching his students to swim. In a methodical manner, he would explain all the necessary ingredients in swimming. "Your head goes like this, thus creating buoyancy; your feet go like this, thus propelling you forward; your arms go like this to steer you. You put it all together and you've got it!" Hearing him explain it made swimming seem as easy as baking a Betty Crocker cake from a mix. You just add water and there you go.

The cerebral approach worked on all of my father's swimming students, most of whom, not coincidentally, grew up to be engineers. I, however, needed something else. I've never been interested in why exactly an airplane can fly; I want to know if the pilot has had enough sleep. In learning to swim, I just wanted to know that I wasn't going to die. My father, however, never quite understood the role of anxiety in my fruitless swimming lessons. He eventually decided that perhaps if he yelled or hurled insults, I might learn more quickly. "You're like a rock! You're hopeless! What's wrong with you?" This method may work wonders in the army, but it didn't work with me. I now had two hurdles to overcome, fear of water and fear of being in the water with my father.

After a couple summers' worth of lessons, I had managed, by age six, to learn nothing, setting an all-time failure record for my father. In hindsight, I believe my ability to dodge all learning opportunities did reveal a certain inner strength, a persistent refusal to be like the others. But the British never appreciated Gandhi's persistence, and my family didn't appreciate mine.

My father eventually decided that we didn't actually have to be in a pool for him to get angry with me for not knowing how to swim. He started to have a somewhat Pavlovian reaction toward me. If anybody used the word "swim," my father would glare at me with a combination of shame and anger, a look that said, "I wish I had kept the receipt." To save face, he had come up with a theory of why I couldn't swim. "She's built like a rock," he'd always say. "She just sinks." This wasn't entirely true. I had never actually let go of my father in the pool, preferring instead to cling to him like a koala on a eucalyptus branch during an earthquake. His determination to peel me off himself matched, but did not exceed, my determination to hold on to him.

Sadly enough, my father stopped talking altogether about his glorious swimming lessons. He knew that no impressive tale could match his one big failure, *moi*. He finally announced to the world, which for us consisted of my aunts, uncles, and cousins, that some people are incapable of swimming. "Firoozeh is one of them," he concluded.

When I was eight years old, we went to Switzerland to visit my aunt Parvine, my mother's sister. Aunt Parvine has always been considered something of a deity in our family because she managed, despite being an Iranian woman of her generation, to become a doctor and to set up a successful practice in Geneva. The woman overcame so many hurdles to reach her dream that she deserves to have her likeness carved in marble. The fact that she actually lives in Switzerland further adds to her allure. Iranians have always considered Switzerland the apogee of civilization: a small, clean country where bus drivers don't have to check for tickets since everyone is so genetically honest. Besides, Switzerland has never particularly welcomed Iranians, thus accruing the magnetism that comes only with repeated rejection.

Aunt Parvine told my father that *she* was going to teach me how to swim. My parents decided to leave me with her one afternoon while she worked her medical magic. It didn't occur to them that perhaps they should stay and watch the swimming lesson. My aunt took me to the deep end of the pool and there, this highly educated woman, whom I had grown up worshiping from afar, let go of me. I sank. Perhaps because of her medical training, or perhaps because she couldn't face the prospect of having to explain to my parents that she had killed their child, Parvine eventually decided to intervene. Moments before I got to see the tunnel with the light at the end and the angels beckoning me to join them, she lifted me out of the water.

My aunt dragged me out of the pool and, doing her best imitation of General Patton in a bad mood, announced that I was hopeless. When my parents joined us, she announced, "Firoozeh is a rock."

News of my European failure soon reached the rest of my relatives, thus cementing my reputation as The One Incapable of Swimming. Oddly enough, no one questioned my aunt's method of instruction; she was, after all, a doctor in Switzerland.

My near-drowning experience brought with it an unexpected ray of hope, like a wildflower blooming in a battlefield: my family was now completely resigned to my inability to swim. My father no longer insulted me; instead, he treated me with pity, since he now assumed that I was missing the chromosome necessary for buoyancy. His pity often led to trips to the toy store, thus proving that I was far smarter than my cousins. I managed to acquire eight new tea sets, while my cousins had merely learned to swim.

Most fruits, if left alone on a tree, eventually do ripen, especially if they're not being yelled at. It was thus that I, at the age of ten, decided that I was finally ready to learn to swim. There was, however, one proviso: I wanted to learn to swim in the sea by myself. I proudly made this announcement to my father, who, once he stopped laughing, said: "You never learned to swim in the pool, so now you want to go drown in the ocean?"

That summer, we headed for our annual weeklong vacation by the Caspian Sea. Because of work commitments, my father was unable to join us. My two brothers, my mother, and my aunt Sedigeh and uncle Abdullah and their four sons, who knew how to swim courtesy of my father, headed north to the Caspian.

Once we arrived, I went straight to the beach. I took a few steps into the water, where a gentle wave lifted me and I started to swim. Simple as that.

When we returned to Abadan, I proudly told my father the news. He did not believe me. He and I headed straight for the pool, where he watched in disbelief. "You, Firoozeh," he said, shaking his head, "are an odd child." "No," I said, "there was nobody yelling at me in the sea."

Years later, when we moved to Newport Beach, I discovered that one of the greatest joys in life is jumping from a boat into the deep, blue Pacific ocean. That was before I discovered snorkeling in the crystal-clear waters of the Bahamas with sea turtles and manta rays swimming around me. Later still, my husband introduced me to the cerulean waters of the Greek islands, where I spent hours swimming with the hot, Mediterranean sun burning on my back. But despite my dips in the many beautiful bodies of water in the world, I have never forgotten that first gentle wave in the Caspian Sea, the one that lifted me and assured me that, yes, the pilot has had enough sleep.

America, Land of the Free

Every Thanksgiving, my extended family and I gather at my cousin Morteza's house. My mother brings her traditional shrimp curry, my aunt Sedigeh brings her lima-bean rice with lamb shanks, and my aunt Fatimeh brings her homemade baklava. All the other relatives prepare their favorite Persian dishes and we place them next to the stuffed turkey with all the trimmings. Everyone then proceeds to catch up on the latest family gossip, which usually involves rumors of impending marriages. Once all rumors have been spread and subsequently denied by all involved parties, we give thanks for our lives here in America and for the good fortune of living close to one another. Then we talk about turkeys.

"Turkeys have no flavor."

"The trimmings are worse."

"Do Americans *like* turkey?"

"I don't think they do."

Meanwhile, all the food, including the turkey and trimmings, gets eaten and we all share the American tradition of feeling more stuffed than the bird. Then it's time for dessert: baklava, fruit, pastries, and pumpkin pie, which we serve with Persian ice cream. With its chunks of cream, roasted pistachios, and aromatic cardamom, Persian ice cream serves as a reminder that Persia was once one of the greatest empires in the world. I believe peace in the Middle East could be achieved if the various leaders held their discussions in front of a giant bowl of Persian ice cream, each leader with his own silver spoon. Political differences would melt with every mouthful.

During our Thanksgiving meal, my father gives thanks for living in a free country where he can vote. I always share gratitude for being able to pursue my hopes and dreams, despite being female. My relatives and I are proud to be Iranian, but we also give tremendous thanks for our lives in America, a nation where freedom reigns.

But although "land of the free" refers to the essential freedoms that make this country the greatest democracy on earth, it could also refer to the abundance of free samples available throughout this great land. In our homeland, people who taste something before they buy it are called shoplifters. Here, a person can taste something, not buy it, and still have the clerk wish him a nice day.

A few months ago, my father mentioned that he had gone out to lunch with his brother Nematollah. I was quite surprised, because my father's idea of eating out is going to his sisters' houses. My two aunts, who live in small, modest homes with tiny kitchens, are always ready to serve whoever drops by around mealtime, a term loosely defined as anywhere between breakfast and bedtime, give or take two hours. Their generosity and genuine delight in feeding others prove my theory that the more modest and impractical the kitchen, the more likely one will be invited to stay for a meal. Show me a fancy house with a top-of-the-line gourmet kitchen, and I'll show you a family that eats out a lot.

"So where did you go?" I asked my father.

"Price Club," he said.

Price Club is a chain of huge warehouses that sells items in large quantities. Toilet paper comes in packages of thirty-six rolls, and one box of muffin mix yields 144 muffins. As far as I know, Price Club has no restaurant. Puzzled, I probed further.

"What did you eat there?"

"Samples," he replied.

Price Club has samples, rows and rows of endless samples. Itching to try the latest frozen chicken burrito or those mini hot dogs that come in mini buns? How about some instant soup, ice-cream sandwiches, spaghetti sauce, or pork buns? It's all there and it's all free. The mind-boggling generosity even extends to second and third helpings. I have witnessed people hanging around the Mrs. Fields sample table far longer than it takes to actually chew one and walk away. These anonymous people who shamelessly eat their way through the store now have a face: my father's.

"So what did you actually eat?" I inquired.

"I don't know," he replied. "It all tasted the same."

Under normal circumstances, my father would not eat a frozen Western-style fish enchilada, but give him a free sample and all rules of judgment and taste are suspended. The same goes for airline food. Once he finishes his own tray, he is more than happy to finish ours. "You're not going to eat that?" he asks, referring to whatever the rest of us have found to be inedible. "Give it to me." My father is every flight attendant's dream, simplifying the stacking process by thoroughly emptying each tray.

A few years ago, my brother Farshid sent my parents on a first-class vacation to Japan. They weren't as impressed by Japan as they were by the food service in first class. My father did admit, though, that he felt ill after the flight. "I ate nonstop," he said.

When my parents returned from their trip, they presented me with, among other gifts, fourteen mini jars of jam.

"What are these from?" I asked.

"Breakfast in the airplane," my mother replied. "We each got two jars."

"What about the other ten jars?" I asked, not wanting to know the answer.

"Those are from the other passengers who didn't want theirs."

I envisioned the first-class passengers, spreading their cloth napkins on their laps, when suddenly, "Doo you vant deh jelly?" My mother, with her thick Middle Eastern accent, could just as easily have asked for their passports, which the passengers would have handed over gladly, just to get rid of her. It is fair to assume that by the time my parents shuffled off the airplane, their pockets laden with a bounty of wrapped sugar cubes and tiny bottles of ketchup, the entire cabin knew that my parents usually fly coach.

My parents' hunting and gathering instincts are not limited to the freebies in first class; they also get their money's worth in coach. My children know that a visit from their grandparents means a dozen packets of American Airlines peanuts. How do they get so many? My mother has a system. "I tell them that I'm visiting my grandkids and they love peanuts." I assume that works better than telling the truth: "I'm paying $150 for this seat and I would like the equivalent in free food."

Evidently, my parents are not the only ones unable to resist the pull of a free meal. Denny's, one of my father's favorite American restaurants, serves free birthday meals. Denny's assumes, of course, that nobody would go to eat a birthday meal alone. It is fair to expect that a person celebrating his birthday would bring along a few paying friends. Of course, there is an exception to every rule, and Kazem is his name.

My father has no idea of his exact birthdate. Whenever a child was born in his family, someone made a notation in the family Koran. The flaw in this system became apparent when someone lost the Koran. My father and his siblings have had to rely on one another's memories to approximate their ages.

"He was born the year of the flood, which makes him seventy-five."

"No, that can't be right. He was born the year I learned how to read, so he's seventy-seven."

"No, he was born the year all the chickens died. He's seventy-one, maybe seventy-two."

When my parents were coming to America, my father had to choose a birthdate. Ever the practical man, he decided on March 18, my mother's birthday. This way, he figured, filling out paperwork would be considerably easier since he would only have to remember one date. His system was flawless until Denny's marketing gurus started offering those free birthday meals. Every March 18, my parents would experience the same scene. "Isn't that adorable?" the waitress always said. "Matching birthdays! Hey, Oscar, check this out!" To get their free chicken-fried steak, my parents had to endure the inquisition.

"How did you two meet?"

"When did you realize you have the same birthday?"

"That is the cutest thing I have ever seen."

Rather than go into the whole "We somehow lost the Koran and that's why we have the same birthday" story, my parents just smiled and hoped the waitress would go away. Eventually, my father decided to go to Denny's alone on his birthday, thus avoiding the entire "Ain't it romantic to have the same birthday?" scenario.

When my father retired, he found himself with lots of free time. Retirement traditionally brings out men's true passions: golfing, fishing, spelunking. Ever since he retired, what was once a mere pastime of my father's has now become a full-time mania that can be summed up in one word: time-shares.

My parents still live in Newport Beach, an affluent community full of tanned, yacht-loving, tennis-playing people named Fritz and Binky. My parents have nothing in common with any other resident of the town. They're not rich, they play no sports, and I'm quite sure that neither one knows how to spell or pronounce "yacht." But they have one thing in common with their neighbors: a ZIP code that means money. My parents are regular targets for marketers looking to sell anything to presumably wealthy retirees. When my father was working, my mother got rid of the nasty telemarketers with a standard response delivered in her thick accent: "I am the maid." Any mail soliciting anything was thrown away before my father came home. All this changed after my father retired. Now a cheerful, eager immigrant greets any marketer who calls the house.

People hawking time-shares are the most insidious, luring their prospective victims with far more than the usual free T-shirt or can opener. They offer everything from a free overnight stay at a nice hotel to a free dinner to a $50 gift certificate. All you have to do is attend one of their "seminars," which are basically long infomercials without the benefit of a mute button. Far better trained than the CIA and more persistent than Hare Krishnas, these salespeople know how to corner their unsuspecting prey and make them sign away their life savings. One minute you're laughing with the nice salesperson, the next minute you own a time-share in Des Moines.

Somehow, my parents survived their first time-share experience without buying anything, but the sales tactics were so forceful that my mother swore she would never go again. My father, the taste of the free filet mignon still lingering in his mouth, wasn't ready to quit. He was upset that my mother did not want to make time-shares a regular part of their twilight years. "Why can't you just go and have a good time?" he asked her. Perhaps the same can be asked of patients going to the dentist for root canals.

Time-share seminars have a certain addictive quality. Unable to convince my mother to join him, my father recruited Uncle Nematollah, who brought with him the added advantage of speaking less English than my mother. This was a good thing, since his inability to understand the sales pitches rendered him far less likely to sign on any dotted line. My uncle just wanted to know when the free lunch would be served.

My father and uncle managed to see Palm Springs for free, twice. "All we had to do was listen to two half-day seminars! It was great!" They also saw San Diego and Santa Barbara courtesy of time-share seminars. They did, of course, give up several days of their life, but, as my uncle said, "I'm recording all the shows we're missing on my VCR!" Once they had honed their skills, their tactics were simple. As my father explained to me, "I just go and tell them I have no money and my brother doesn't understand English."

Sadly enough, my uncle Nematollah recently decided to return to Iran. This departure has left my father without a partner in crime. Despite his persistence, his sisters refuse to join him because, frankly, they're too smart. My father, never one to give up hope, recently announced that he is trying to convince my mother to give time-shares another chance. "If she understood less English, she would enjoy the seminars a lot more," he told me. In the meantime, he has a lot more time for his other hobby, watching television, which, unlike yachting, fishing, or spelunking, is completely free.

The Ham Amendment

One of my father's favorite foods is ham. This is not a problem if your name is Bob and you live in Alabama. But when you're Kazem living in Abadan, satisfying your ham cravings can be a challenge.

During my childhood, Iran was a monarchy led by the Shah. His picture was everywhere. The serious expression on his face made it clear that this was an important person having important thoughts. His beautiful wife, Farah, was usually seen standing beside him in photos, wearing a large, bejeweled crown, which appeared rather uncomfortable but managed to make her, too, look far more important than the average person walking down the street. They had four children, all of whom were envied by the entire Iranian population for leading perfect lives, lives which included French-speaking nannies, skiing lessons, fancy clothes, and the assumption of perpetual happiness. I didn't really think much about the royal family, except I had noticed that they owned a lot of big jewelry. My parents, however, were huge fans. My father firmly believed that the Shah would educate and modernize Iran. After his graduate years in Texas, my father had returned to Iran full of American optimism. With its vast oil reserves and abundance of smart people, Iran, according to my father, could really go places.

When I was five years old, the Shah was scheduled to come to Abadan for the inauguration of a petrochemical plant. A parade had been arranged and a special float had been built for him. To avoid the large crowds, we decided to skip the parade, knowing that we would not be able to see anything. We were not, however, willing to miss our only opportunity for a brush with royalty. My father, a man whose engineering mind always comes up with a solution, devised a plan. On a scorching hot day, the day *before* the parade, my mother wore her Jackie Kennedy sleeveless dress, my brothers put on long-sleeved shirts and ties, and the five of us drove to the parade site in my father's air-conditioned Chevrolet. Granted, there was no parade, no cheering crowd, no music, and, least of all, no royalty. But none of that mattered. We climbed on the beribboned float intended for the Shah, our faces protected by the awning built to shield the royal face from the blazing sun. We smiled. My father's camera captured *our* royal moment.

What brought the Shah to Abadan was its seemingly endless oil supply. This natural gift was a mixed blessing, a bit like having a garden that stands out in the entire neighborhood. You know that, eventually, somebody's going to come and pick your flowers while you're sleeping. In our case, it was the British who came for the oil.

The British were the first to realize the huge financial potential of the vast Iranian oil reserves. With the sound of cash registers ringing in its executives' ears, British Petroleum negotiated an agreement with the Iranian government that allowed the British to drill for and sell the oil in exchange for a small sum. In a perfect world, the kindergarten teacher would have stood up before any documents were signed and said, "Time out for Britain. We'll renegotiate after a nap." But alas, with no teacher present to remind the participants of the universal concept of fairness, the British applied a different universal concept, greed. The agreement between British Petroleum and the government of Iran was destined for disaster.

Fortunately, exploitation has a limited shelf life, and Iranians eventually woke up. In the early 1950s, the prime minister, Dr. Muhammad Mossadegh, nationalized Iran's oil. The British were forced to leave Iran. Unwilling to simply walk away from their golden-egg-laying goose, the foreign oil companies banded together and boycotted Iranian oil, resulting in a huge economic downturn. Within two years after the nationalization of its oil, the Iranian economy lay in shambles. Political upheaval ensued. Once again, Iran was ripe for foreign exploitation. This time, with foreign powers working behind the scene, Dr. Mossadegh, the national hero, was ousted. History partly repeated itself, and the foreign oil companies once again took over the operation and exploitation of the Iranian oil industry. This time, however, Iran received a larger portion of the profits and more control over oil operations.

By the time I was born in Abadan in 1965, there was no longer a large British population in town. A few foreigners remained, all employed by the operating companies. Iran was finally reaping most of the profits from its own oil.

In the absence of the British, the residents of Abadan benefited from a city built by thoughtful British planners. We had swimming pools, clubhouses, and very orderly housing developments. My hometown looked different from any other Iranian city.

Catering to the European expatriates, some stores in Abadan carried foreign foods, exotic products such as Ovaltine, Kit Kat candy bars, and ham. Even with the British gone, their canned and boxed foods remained in the stores, serving as a reminder of the exotic world that existed outside our borders.

During his graduate years in America, my father had been deprived of his beloved Persian food—no steaming platters of saffron-infused rice, no tender chicken kebobs, no marinated lamb shanks with eggplant stew. Exhibiting the survival instinct of adaptation, he had developed a taste for cafeteria food, in particular Jell-O and ham. After his return to Iran and subsequent marriage, he had convinced my mother to make Jell-O on a fairly regular basis. I liked the wiggly stuff, but I preferred to eat the powder raw out of the palm of my hand.

My father's ham cravings, however, were a different story. My mother would not touch the stuff with a ten-meter pole. She cringed at even the word *jambon,* the French word used in Iran for ham. I had no idea why my mother reacted so strongly. All I knew was that whenever my father wanted to buy ham, I was his chosen partner. And I was honored. The opportunity to spend time alone with my father was so rare that I would have done just about anything to have him all to myself. Had he wanted to rob a bank, I would happily have driven the getaway car.

Unlike the Persian markets, where the fruits and vegetables were openly displayed, the tiny grocery stores that sold ham carried foods veiled in boxes and cans. Pictures hinted at the contents, although there was no rooster in the cornflakes. An air of mystery hung around these exotic foreign products, many of which had pictures of smiling people on the containers. None of the people looked Iranian, which led me to the obvious conclusion that there were a lot of happy people living in other countries.

Once the ham was purchased, my father and I rode home, sharing the excitement felt by cavemen who had successfully hunted the elusive mammoth. My mother and brothers stayed away from the kitchen while my father meticulously prepared his meal with fresh tomatoes, pickles, and onions. He then sat down to savor every mouthful while I watched him. Eating his beloved *jambon* always put him in a good mood, which then led to stories about America and his exciting graduate years. I never asked to eat the ham and my dad never offered. Having been part of the hunt was satisfying enough for me.

When I started first grade, I began studying Islam in school one hour per week. We studied the history of Judaism, Christianity, and Islam. We learned about the Prophet Muhammad and the imams. All the stories were marvelous—until the lecture about forbidden foods. To my complete shock, I discovered that my own father was destined to a *very bad place* for a *very long time*. All of a sudden, our ham excursions no longer seemed fun and innocent. I now understood why my mother wouldn't even look at the stuff. She was trying to save her soul.

I rushed home that day with an assignment far more important than my math homework. I was determined to alter the course of my father's afterlife.

As soon as my father's car turned into our driveway, I ran out and told him of the unpleasant future that awaited him, forever. He let out a hearty laugh. I started to cry. Once my father saw my tears, he sat down with me and said, "Firoozeh, when the Prophet Muhammad forbade ham, it was because people did not know how to cook it properly and many people became sick as a result of eating it. The Prophet, who was a kind and gentle man, wanted to protect people from harm, so he did what made sense at the time. But now, people know how to prepare ham safely, so if the Prophet were alive today, he would change that rule."

He continued, "It's not what we eat or don't eat that makes us good people; it's how we treat one another. As you grow older, you'll find that people of every religion think they're the best, but that's not true. There are good and bad people in every religion. Just because someone is Muslim, Jewish, or Christian doesn't mean a thing. You have to look and see what's in their hearts. That's the only thing that matters, and that's the only detail God cares about."

I was six years old and I knew that I had just been made privy to something very big and important, something far larger than the jewels in the Shah's crown, something larger than my little life in Abadan. My father's words felt scandalous, yet utterly and completely true.

In the midst of my thoughtfulness, I heard my father continue, "And when you're older, Firoozeh, I'll have you try something really delicious: grilled lobster."

Treasure Island

When he was growing up in Ahwaz, one of my father's greatest joys was going to the movies. Had it been up to him, he would have happily spent his entire childhood in front of the big screen, dreaming his life away. But movies require a ticket, and tickets cost money.

My father's father, Javad, owned wheat fields outside Ahwaz. When it rained, the wheat grew and there was money for movies, sometimes three in one month. When it didn't rain, which was often in Ahwaz's arid climate, money was scarce. My father grew up looking at clouds and always hoping for rain.

Because there was no air conditioning, movies were shown outdoors in the summer. This meant that certain risk-taking people, like my uncle Muhammad, could climb on high walls and rooftops to watch the movies for free. My father, having inherited the cautious and law-abiding genes in the family, could never quite gather the courage to join his older brother on these free movie escapades, even though he really, really wanted to see the films. His older brother finally persuaded him to live a little and join him on his favorite wall for a night at the movies. My father gave in. Just as the two of them were nesting comfortably, along came a police officer. My uncle Muhammad immediately jumped down and ran away, leaving my panic-stricken father abandoned like a fledgling on a high branch.

The policeman, waving his stick, yelled at my father to get down or else. Trembling, he closed his eyes and jumped right into a pile of bricks. He ran away, bleeding all the way home. The deep gash in his shin eventually became infected, and my father was told he might end up losing his lower leg. After six months, the cut finally healed, but it left behind a scar that is still visible.

The movie theater showed a different film every week. There were the Egyptian movies, usually involving a lovelorn couple; an obstacle in the guise of a mean father, a jealous neighbor, or an illness; and the eventual death of one of the lovers. My father hated these tearjerkers, because no matter how hard he tried to resist, he inevitably left the theater in tears. His favorites were the American Westerns, where the good guys always won. He also loved *Tarzan*, a movie so popular that it had to be shown for several weeks in a row. But my father's all-time favorite movie was the 1934 *Treasure Island*. After seeing that movie, he decided that his goal was to find a treasure, something that would alter the course of his life forever. And this he did.

The treasure he found was not buried, but rather taped on a wall. It was a poster announcing a competition for Fulbright grants. At the time, my father was twenty-three years old and teaching mathematics and engineering in Abadan. He immediately filled out the form and started dreaming about studying in America. One of his colleagues shattered his fantasies by telling him that Fulbright grants were only for the sons of senators and other rich people: "You don't stand a chance, Kazem." My father was ready to abandon his dreams and end the application process, except that he had already asked his boss for a day off to take the Fulbright exam and he was afraid that if he skipped the exam, his boss would think that he had lied just to get a day of vacation. So he, along with hundreds of others thirsting for an education abroad, took the exam. When the results were announced, my father's name was first on the list of people who had passed.

My father, however, was still convinced that in the end, he would be passed over for the son of a rich family. When he was asked to make a choice of schools in America, he said it didn't matter. He just wanted somewhere warm like Ahwaz that had a farming program, since he figured that animals spoke the same language everywhere, even in America. He also said he wanted to study engineering.

A few months later, six of his colleagues received news that they had been awarded Fulbrights.

My father's classes ended for summer vacation and he accepted an engineering position.

A month later, during a trip to the post office, the postal clerk informed my father that he had received a letter about a month earlier that could not be delivered. Apparently, the letter was addressed to the school, but since my father was no longer teaching, the post office had not delivered it. The clerk handed my father an envelope. It was his acceptance letter to Texas A&M, courtesy of a Fulbright grant, along with a scholarship from the Ford Foundation. The letter stated that he was expected in Texas by a certain date for a forty-day orientation program. My father looked at the calendar. That certain date had been a week ago.

Frantic, he ran to his boss and asked for five days off. Having never set foot outside Iran, he needed to go to Tehran to obtain a passport. He didn't quit his job, fearing that having missed the orientation, he might have lost the scholarship.

In Tehran, he headed straight to the passport office and handed the administrator his identification booklet. The administrator leafed through it, handed it back to my father, and said, "I'm sorry. There's a page missing." Sure enough, the last page, the death certificate, was missing. "But I'm alive!" my father pleaded. No matter. He was told he had to obtain another identification booklet, a process that takes three months.

My father's five-day trip to Tehran turned into a twenty-five-day stay, during which he ran around frantically recounting his story to everyone, hoping that someone might know someone who might be able to expedite the process. A kind administrator finally decided to help, supplying him with an identification booklet within a week. He then obtained a passport. Next stop was the American embassy, where he was issued a visa within a couple of hours.

He then returned to Abadan, quit his job, bid a teary good-bye to his sister Sedigeh and her family, and boarded a plane bound for Texas. By the time he arrived in Austin, he had already missed thirty-five days of the forty-day orientation.

For the remaining five days, he was assigned to a room with a Japanese student who found Americans morally bankrupt. For five days, my father listened to his roommate pontificate on the dangers of their new loose surroundings. On the last night of orientation, during the farewell dinner, one student became completely drunk, draped a tablecloth over his body, and danced wildly on the tables. He was hauled away by the organizers, but not before my father recognized the wild and crazy guy as his roommate.

Throughout the school year, my father studied on weekdays;

on weekends, he studied some more. The combination of being shy, not knowing English well, and missing most of the orientation proved to be a recipe for loneliness. During one long weekend, another of the Fulbright students barged into my father's room and announced that he could no longer take the loneliness and would be abandoning his studies to return home. My father tried to dissuade him, but in view of Kazem's thick accent and his unique flair with the English language, it's anybody's guess what actually came out of his mouth. Anyway, the student went back home.

A few days later, my father noticed a large envelope addressed to the departed student. Accidentally opening other people's mail has always been one of my father's favorite hobbies. The envelope contained a letter from the Fulbright office letting the student know that he could transfer to any school he chose, and that any accommodation would be made to ensure a memorable experience. This gave my father a brilliant idea.

He decided he wanted to transfer to another school with a livelier environment, but he didn't want to ask directly for a transfer. He wanted the committee to suggest it. So he painstakingly wrote a letter describing how lonely he was. The Fulbright office responded immediately, telling him that he had been assigned an American hostess who would show him around town on weekends. This is not what my father had had in mind.

The following Saturday, he found himself standing in the lobby of an art museum. His hostess had obviously thought that as an engineering student, my father could benefit from a bit of culture. Little did she know that the only culture my father was interested in was the kind in yogurt. My one memory of a family excursion to an art museum ended with my father asking, "Did we have to *pay* to get into this place?"

After half a dozen culturally enriching weekends, my father decided that the merits of loneliness were highly underrated. Given the choice between spending time with a kind soul who had given up her weekends for some engineer from a country she had never heard of, or reading, say, theories about fluid mechanics, his decision was obvious. My father informed the Fulbright office that, thank you very much, he had been cured of his loneliness.

A few weeks before spring vacation, one of my father's engineering professors asked him if he had any plans to go away for Easter break. He did not. So the professor invited my father to accompany him and another professor to Princeton, New Jersey. Having noticed my father's passion for math and engineering, as well as his tendency to spend long stretches of time alone, they had thought he might want to come along. My father happily accepted, knowing that this was going to be much better than hanging out in art museums. During the long car drive, the professors explained that they would be having a reunion with an old acquaintance. They had attended a seminar taught by this remarkable man years ago and had decided to pay him another visit.

After three days of driving, they arrived in New Jersey. The next day, with my father in tow, the two professors headed to meet their teacher. The year was 1953.

Albert Einstein possessed, according to my father, deep, penetrating eyes; he spoke in a deliberate and gentle manner. One of the professors introduced the Fulbright scholar from Iran. Professor Einstein asked my father to tell him a little bit about the Fulbright program, the key words here being "little bit." My father told him about the history of the grants and how Senator Fulbright had started them after World War II as a means of fostering understanding between the United States and other countries. Kazem said he hadn't believed that a teacher in Abadan would be selected for such a prestigious grant, even though he really was qualified. He told Einstein he had always dreamed of studying in America; how wonderful everything was! And that was just the beginning.

Here was a lonely foreigner who had basically spent an entire year not talking to anyone but who had suddenly decided to spring a year's allotment of conversation on an unsuspecting genius. One can only imagine what was going through Albert Einstein's brilliant mind: "Never ask about Fulbrights again."

Once the soliloquy was completed, Kazem asked Professor Einstein if he knew anything about Iran. He was looking for an excuse to segue into his scintillating speech on the petroleum industry in Iran—its past, its present, and its future. But God was clearly smiling on Albert Einstein, who unintentionally threw Kazem for a loop. "I know about your famous carpets and your beautiful cats." That put an end to the conversation since my father had no idea what he meant by these "beautiful cats," and was not about to ask. When trying to impress the likes of Albert Einstein, one pretends to know what the genius is talking about, especially when it pertains to the country one is representing thanks to a Fulbright grant. So my father said what he always says when he has no idea what the other person is talking about: "Yes, yes."

My father returned to Texas a much happier man. His meeting with Albert Einstein had confirmed his suspicion that anything is possible in America. He spent the next few months finishing his studies and getting ready to return to Abadan, where he looked forward to feeling once again the warmth and kindness of his siblings.

He was, however, returning with more than just a diploma. He also had a new dream, in which the treasure was no longer buried. He dreamed that someday, he would return to America with his own children. And they, the children of an engineer from Abadan, would have access to the same educational opportunities as anybody else, even the sons of senators and the rich. It was a dream that my brothers and I were honored to fulfill.

It's All Relatives

It's said that Inuits have more than twenty words for "snow." This seems logical given that the average Alaskan spends a lifetime surrounded by snow, observing details that the rest of us have never noticed.

Having spent my adolescence in Newport Beach, I learned the many nuances of "tan." I learned the difference between a deep tan, a fading tan, a bronze tan, and a new tan. No one would be caught dead with a farmer's tan, which is a tan showing the outline of a T-shirt and shorts. Even worse is a fake 'n' bake, one acquired in a tanning booth. A surfer's tan is the most desirable, since it also comes with sun-bleached hair.

Growing up in Iran, I was surrounded not by snow or tanned people, but by relatives. Not surprisingly, my native language, Persian, contains many more precise words for relatives than does the English language. My father's brothers are my *amoo*. My mother's brother is a *dye-yee*. My aunts' husbands are either *shohar ammeh* or *shohar khaleh*, depending on which side of the family they are from. In English, all these men are simply my "uncles." Only one word describes their children in English, "cousin," whereas in Persian, we have eight words to describe the exact relationship of each cousin.

When we lived in Abadan, we lived near my father's oldest sister, Sedigeh. She is my *ameh*, my father's sister. Her four sons are my *pessar ameh*, "sons of father's sister." Our families spent every free moment together and I always thought of my aunt Sedigeh and uncle Abdullah as a second set of parents. Since my aunt Sedigeh never had a daughter, she regarded me as her own. Always warm and affectionate, she showered me with compliments that stayed with me long after our visits had ended. She often told me that I was smart and patient and that she wished that I were her daughter. She never criticized me, but loved me as only a father's sister could. To me, the word *ameh* still conjures up feelings of being enveloped with love.

Aunt Sedigeh also had a beautiful garden full of nasturtiums, roses, snapdragons, and sweet peas, a veritable Disneyland for the olfactory sense. We went to her house for lunch every Friday; while the smells of her cooking filled the house, I would go in her garden and smell every flower over and over again. Even though I went there weekly, each visit to her garden was as exciting as the first.

When we moved to America, I no longer had access to those fragrances and I forgot all about my aunt's garden. Strolling through a market in Berkeley one day, I spotted a vaguely familiar flower. I bent down and smelled a sweet pea for the first time in fifteen years. Suddenly, I was six years old again and running around chasing butterflies in my aunt's garden.

After lunch at my aunt's house, the adults napped and I embarked on my favorite adventure, going into my uncle Abdullah's library. Uncle Abdullah, my *shohar ameh*, was a man of books, a learned man who enjoyed learning for its own sake. Fluent in Arabic, he had a particular interest in linguistic roots. In his thirst for knowledge, he stood alone. Potatoes, radishes, and turnips were the only roots my family cared about. I, however, was fascinated by his interest in words, although I could never understand his explanations. If I asked him the meaning of a word in Persian, he would explain its Arabic etymology, giving endless examples of words sharing the same root. He would then discuss the word's evolution into its present form and throw in a few quotes from the Koran for good measure. By the time my uncle finished explaining, I had usually forgotten my question. Nonetheless, I was entirely fascinated by his passion for words and by how *much* he knew.

In my uncle's library, I always headed straight for the collected *Reader's Digests*, which I liked for two reasons: they were small and they arrived in the mail every month from America. I did not know a word of English, yet I enjoyed studying the child-size magazines from cover to cover, trying to figure out what the stories were about. I always made sure to put them back in the exact order in which I had found them, for fear of losing the privilege of browsing in my uncle's library. Years later, after we moved to America, my father bought me my own subscription to *Reader's Digest*, an event that remains the high point of my life in junior high.

Aunt Sedigeh and Uncle Abdullah now live near my parents in Southern California. Even though their condominium has only a tiny garden, they have managed to cultivate an enviable cornucopia of figs, pomegranates, sweet lemons, and herbs. My aunt is still a wonderful cook and no visit to Southern California would ever be complete without her lentil saffron rice, her eggplant stew with beef shank, or her signature oven-cooked salmon stuffed with homegrown herbs. My sweet *ameh* still delivers her kind compliments, but nowadays she tells me what a good mother I am, and I tell her what a compliment that is coming from her.

Uncle Abdullah is a translator, a job that allows him to surround himself with his beloved words. His passions, however, have broadened to include computers, which he discovered when he was well into his seventies. This means that whenever my husband, the software engineer, visits Southern California, he spends hours with Abdullah, trying to retrieve lost and deleted files.

"I don't know how it happened," my uncle always says.

My husband reminds him, "When the computer asks, 'Are you *sure* you want to delete this file?,' just say no."

"It doesn't ask me," my uncle always replies. "They just disappear."

My aunt and uncle have four sons, Muhammad, Mahmood, Mehdi, and Mehrdad, all of whom are married with children of their own. Even though my father considers all his nieces and nephews to be his own kids, he is particularly close to his sister Sedigeh's children because they lived near us in Abadan, allowing my father the pleasure of watching his nephews grow up. He loves recounting endless stories about each one, emphasizing their unusual intelligence, wit, and charm. "We've already heard that one," we tell him, but my father never hears us, for in recounting his stories, he relives the sweetest moments of his life. In return, his nephews adore him.

When my parents want to go on a great vacation, they visit Mehdi, who is a professor in Austria. "Mehdi knows how to show us a good time," they always say. When they want any kind of medical advice, they ask Mahmood, the orthopedic surgeon— "the best surgeon ever," according to them. When my parents want hospitality, they visit Muhammad, whose kindness and generosity remind my parents of their lives back in Abadan. And for entertainment, they always visit Mehrdad, who is their unofficial third son and the proud father of the only two redheaded members of our family. "His kids could be models," boast my parents.

After the Iranian Revolution, my father, unable to find a job in Southern California, had stayed with Mehdi's family while working in Northern California. Mehdi's oldest son, Darius, and Darius's younger brother, Ryan, had moved into one room so that my father could have his own room. Twenty years later, my husband and I cleared out a room in our house so Darius could stay with us while working as an intern at a nearby computer firm. "I guess it's payback time," he said when he arrived. We all laughed, knowing that the thread of kindness and generosity in our family has no beginning and no end. "Just make sure you have room in *your* house," I told Darius. "Someday, my kids will be coming."

When Darius's grandmother Sedigeh was a young girl, she was, according to my father, "the smartest one of all." Times being what they were, Sedigeh was not allowed to pursue her education past sixth grade and was married shortly thereafter. All her brothers became engineers and doctors. My father found this a huge injustice. He always told me that if his sister had been able to pursue her education, she would have become the best doctor of them all, for not only was she smart, she was resourceful as well. He loved to tell the story of how one year, all the family's chickens were dying and nobody knew why. Sedigeh was determined to find the cause. She began to observe the chickens closely and noticed that they appeared to have trouble swallowing. She then performed an autopsy on one of the dead chicks and discovered a tumor in its throat. She then took each chick that was still alive, made a small incision in its throat, removed the tumor, and sewed it back up. They all survived.

Whenever my father told me this story, his eyes welled up. "What an injustice to deny a mind like that an education," he always said, his voice getting smaller and smaller, before he exclaimed: "And you, Firoozeh, will go to a university!" My father could not change the past, but the past had most certainly changed him. "I don't care if you do nothing with your college diploma, but you will have one!" he adamantly declared. It was payback time for my father, whose daughter was destined to claim the education denied his sister.

My oldest paternal uncle, Muhammad, did become a doctor, the first in the family. As a young doctor, he supported his younger siblings, enabling them to continue their education. My *amoo* had a successful practice in Ahwaz and enjoyed a life of luxury up until the Iranian Revolution. He and his family fled to America in 1980 with just a few belongings. Muhammad's Iranian medical license did not allow him to practice in America, so he had to take both English and medical courses and pass the necessary exams. At fifty-eight, an age when most doctors are thinking of retirement, my uncle had to spend a year as an intern, the oldest one in the hospital.

After completing his education, he set up a practice in Southern California, joining the ranks of other hardworking immigrants pursuing the American dream. Eventually, he managed to create a lifestyle somewhat like the one he left in Iran. He even bought a Mercedes, which, unlike his Mercedes in Iran, he has to drive himself.

My father always says that his brother made the family proud twice, once as a young man when he became a doctor and once as a not-so-young man when he became a doctor for the second time. Uncle Muhammad is our family's symbol of perseverance.

All of my *ameh* and *amoo* live within fifteen minutes of one another and manage to get together for every possible occasion, from birthdays to that long-standing favorite, the Miss America pageant. My *amoo* Muhammad recently turned eighty, an event that the family celebrated with a Hawaiian-themed birthday party. Seventy family members spanning three generations attended. Uncle Muhammad gave a speech and announced that he would never retire. The family cheered.

As boring as graduation ceremonies are, my relatives attend every one, rejoicing in the academic accomplishments of the children and grandchildren. Nobody understands the graduation speeches, but everyone goes to clap and cheer. Like all Iranians, we consider academics to be of the utmost importance. Almost every child in my extended family has attended college, a record that brings tears of pride and joy to the eyes of the older generation, a record that we hope to continue.

My relatives also attend one another's housewarming parties, New Year's celebrations, and baby showers, all en masse. Recently, my *pessar amoo*, the son of my father's brother, moved into an apartment near UCLA to begin dental school. His father threw him a housewarming party, and fifty members of the family showed up to celebrate in his tiny apartment. "It was great!" my father said.

My father and his siblings drive one another to doctor appointments and pick one another up from the airport. If one goes for a checkup, they all call for the results. They know which one of them has high blood pressure and which one is allergic to dairy products. They know one another's favorite foods and often use the knowledge to lure one another for visits. "Kazem, I just made rice pudding" is my aunt Sedigeh's way of inviting my father over. His other sister, Fatimeh, has her own equally effective siren song: "Kazem, the mulberries are ripe."

Together, my relatives form an alliance that represents a genuine and enduring love of family, one that sustains them through difficulties and gives them reasons to celebrate during good times. My father and his siblings have even purchased burial plots together because, as my father told me, "we never want to be separated." Uncle Muhammad, the oldest doctor, purchased a plot high on the hill with a view of the Pacific Ocean. "I've always wanted an ocean view," he says.

Before I married François, I told him that I came with a tribe—a free set of Ginsu knives with every purchase, so to speak. François said he loved tribes, especially mine. Now, whenever we visit my relatives, all of whom dote on my husband, I realize that he didn't marry me despite my tribe, he married me *because* of them. Without my relatives, I am but a thread; together, we form a colorful and elaborate Persian carpet.

Me and Bob Hope

The great American philosopher Dr. Seuss once wrote about a fellow named the Grinch, who for some mysterious reason did not enjoy Christmas. Dr. Seuss tried to delve deep into the unfestive mind of this enigmatic creature in order to find a possible reason for his lack of Christmas spirit:

> It could be his head wasn't screwed on just right.
> It could be, perhaps, that his shoes were too tight.

These are fine explanations, but to me the obvious answer was overlooked. Perhaps the Grinch was, like me, a Muslim, someone who was left out of all Christmas festivities. The problem with the religious explanation is obvious: nothing rhymes with "Muslim." At least if you're "Jewish," you can feel "blue-ish" during Christmas, but with "Muslim" you're just stuck.

When I lived in Iran, the country was predominantly, but not entirely Muslim. Iranian Jews and Christians worshiped in peace. My family and I were secular Muslims, like most of the population. My parents' idea of being religious consisted of donating a part of their income to the poor and not eating ham. The only women who chose to cover themselves head to toe with a *chador* were either older women or villagers. In the cities, Iranian woman preferred to dress like Jackie Kennedy or Elizabeth Taylor.

In school, one of the subjects we studied was religion. We learned not only about Islam but also about Judaism, Christianity, and Buddhism. We were taught to practice Islam, but to respect all religions. Knowledge of Islam was mandatory for all Muslim students; its practice was not. The Christian and Jewish children at my school were exempt from religious studies, a fact that caused much envy among the rest of us.

When we moved to America, I discovered that school was much more fun here. There was less homework, no endless math drills, and no memorization of famous poems. I loved my teacher, Mrs. Sandberg. I loved Girl Scouts, the Whittier Public Library, and Butterfinger candy bars. I loved Halloween, *The Brady Bunch,* and free toys in cereal boxes. It seemed to me that life in America was one long series of festivities, all of them celebrated with merriment and chocolate.

The laughter, however, stopped when we reached Christmas. All of a sudden, everyone was having a party and *I* was not invited.

In Iran, the biggest holiday is Nowruz, New Year's Day. Since it is a secular holiday, Nowruz is celebrated by the entire country, as Thanksgiving is in the United States. It always begins on the first day of spring at the exact moment of the equinox. This means that every year Nowruz begins at a different time. One year it might be March 21 at 5:32 A.M., while the next year it might occur on March 20 at 11:54 P.M. Every Iranian knows the exact moment the jubilation begins.

The festivities are preceded by weeks of preparation. Everyone thoroughly cleans his house, buys or makes new clothes, and bakes traditional pastries. A ceremonial setting called a *haft-seen*, which consists of seven symbols beginning with the sound "s," is displayed along with other meaningful objects like a mirror, colored eggs, and goldfish in a bowl. The objects represent health, renewal, prosperity, fertility, and the usual universal hopes shared by people at any New Year's celebration. Unlike the traditional American New Year's wishes, however, the Persian New Year holds no symbols of hope representing "losing ten pounds" or "getting in shape."

For Nowruz, most businesses close and the streets are deserted. For twelve days after the equinox, people visit relatives and friends, always starting with the eldest. Once all the elders have been visited, they in turn visit the younger members of the family. At every house, a tray of homemade sweets is offered along with wishes for the New Year. Children receive money, always in the form of brand-new bills. I assume that since the wave of immigration after 1980, banks in America have noticed a sudden increase in demand for crisp bills in the month of March.

But when we moved to America in 1972, Nowruz lost all its meaning. No longer did we feel the excitement building toward the big day. No longer did we see people cleaning their drapes, buying new clothes, or sweeping their yards spotless. No longer did we prepare for an onslaught of visitors. Gone were the smells of pastries coming from every kitchen, gone were the purple hyacinths that decorated every house, gone were the strangers wishing us *"Nowruz Mubarak,"* "Happy New Year." Gone was the excitement in the air.

In America, we have tried our best to celebrate Nowruz, but it's a challenge. Since it's not an American holiday, everyone is either at work or in school. It's hard to get in the mood when your national holiday falls somewhere between soccer practice and the dentist appointment. However, now that there are more Iranian immigrants in America, it is becoming far more enjoyable to celebrate Nowruz. I'm sure that Macy's Nowruz sale is not too far behind.

In America, Christmas is the king of all holidays. To be left out of Christmas is the ultimate minority experience. As an adolescent, I learned to commiserate with my Jewish friends. Together, we talked about how we couldn't wait for December 26, how we hated hearing Christmas songs everywhere, and how we wished that our mothers would, just once, bake us Christmas cookies. Although I enjoyed kvetching with my Jewish friends, I was not convinced that they could thoroughly feel my pain. They, after all, had Hanukkah, which, even though it's completely different from Christmas, still involves food, clothing, presents, and light. At my house, December could have just as easily been August, since there was absolutely no sign of any festivities. Christmas vacation was a long, boring holiday.

In Iran, whenever we had free time, we got together with relatives. In America, whenever we had free time, we watched television. Christmas for us meant an evening spent with Bob Hope, John Denver, Sonny and Cher, Tony Orlando and Dawn, and any other celebrity who managed to have a Christmas special. We weren't picky. If it was on, we watched. My parents, however, had a particular fondness for the annual Bob Hope Christmas specials with frequent guest star Brooke Shields. They didn't understand any of Bob's jokes, but my father laughed along with the laugh tracks. Then my father would ask, "What did he say?" And that was how I spent Christmas Eve—translating Bob Hope's jokes into Persian, jokes that my parents didn't understand in any language. Of course, for my father, Bob Hope was more than just a comedian; he was a dignified older man who wore sharp suits, had great posture, and managed to be witty without ever getting nervous. I think that secretly my father wanted to be Bob Hope.

My mother thought Brooke Shields, in the dozen different outfits she wore for each show, was the embodiment of perfection. I could not understand why Brooke, who is the same age as I am, never went through an awkward adolescent stage. I wished I could be Brooke Shields. So did my mom.

In between all the song-and-dance numbers, we watched endless commercials for all the wonderful gifts that we were not going to receive and made plans for the after-Christmas sales, a celebration that unites all religions.

During the month of December, people constantly wished us "Merry Christmas" in that automatic way. If we said that we didn't celebrate Christmas, we received a cheery "Happy Hanukkah." Call us Scrooge, but we didn't celebrate that one either.

"Then what *do* you celebrate?" we were always asked.

"Nothing," we'd say.

"What *are* you?"

"Muslim."

A few brave souls inquired further, usually academic types or residents of Berkeley. The average citizen, however, smiled, said, "Oh," and left.

When I married a Catholic, I became a card-carrying member of the Christmas Club. Now, every December, my children and I drag a tree into our house, leaving a trail of pine needles should the tree need to find its way back. We decorate the tree with ornaments that take up half of our closet space, eat Christmas cookies that help us grow in both spirit and girth, and read Christmas stories that leave my children asking questions like

"How can Santa not bring toys for some kids when, Mommy, you told us that all kids are good inside?"

Despite my dislike for cleaning pine needles from every nook and cranny, I love celebrating Christmas. I love watching my children count the days till December 25, a countdown that seems to get harder every year. I remember when having to wait a week for Nowruz felt like an eternity. And, just as my father assured me that Nowruz was indeed around the corner, I assure my kids that Christmas will be here before they know it.

Even though I'm too old to believe in Santa Claus, I'm just the right age for baking Christmas cookies. What's Christmas without bourbon balls, gingerbread, and fudge? I'm not sure which I enjoy more, the flavors or the smells, but either way, they remind me of the excitement of Nowruz. My Christmas kitchen smells of ginger, chocolate, and cinnamon. In my childhood kitchen, Nowruz smelled of cardamom, roasted pistachios, and rose water. And in every Iranian living room, the sweet scent of hyacinths trumpeted the arrival of Nowruz and the beginning of spring. In America, our Christmas tree fills our house with the unmistakable aroma of pine, a scent I now associate with winter celebrations.

Despite my new love for Christmas, I often find myself exhausted at the end of December. Christmas, with its elf laborers and flying reindeer, is far more complicated than Nowruz. In between all the cooking and cleaning, I try my best to answer my children's many questions. I do my best to explain how Santa manages to deliver so many presents in just one night and how he manages not to trip anyone's burglar alarm and how it is that Santa doesn't have a bad back even though he's an old man and he has to carry so much stuff.

At times like this, I yearn for the simpler days of yore, when

Christmas meant watching Bob Hope sing his version of "White Christmas" as my parents and I slumped on the sofa in our summer clothes in the warm Newport Beach weather.

Now every Christmas Eve, when the kids are finally in bed, the dishes are washed, and the log is on its final breath, I can't help but think of Bob Hope and wonder if he realizes that in my childhood home, he was *way* bigger than Santa Claus. Mr. Hope, unlike the bearded fellow, came to *everyone's* house. And even though my parents didn't understand any of his jokes, I got them all. And they were funny, in both English and Persian. So, Mr. Hope, thank you and Merry Christmas to all, and to all a good night.

Ï Ran and Ï Ran and Ï Ran

In 1977, the Shah and his wife were scheduled to come to America to meet the newly elected president, Jimmy Carter. Very few Iranians lived in America then, and those of us who did were invited to go to Washington, D.C., to welcome the Shah. The Iranian government would cover all expenses.

My father accepted the invitation. My brothers reacted with a few choice words.

"Are you completely crazy?"

"Haven't you heard about the anti-Shah demonstrators?"

"You'll definitely get beaten up."

"Don't go."

My brothers clearly did not understand the lure of the phrase "all-expense-paid trip."

A few weeks later, drinking fresh-squeezed orange juice in our first-class seats, my parents and I looked forward to our first visit to the nation's capital. During our three-night stay, we were supposed to show up at two events welcoming the Shah. The rest of the time was our own. My father had promised to take me to at least one museum. My mother looked forward to seeing the famous sights.

We arrived at our hotel to find the lobby full of Iranians. Unaccustomed to seeing so many of our fellow countrymen in one place, my parents started mingling feverishly, discovering friends of friends and long-forgotten colleagues. As we went to find our room, we felt like a bunch of kids on a field trip.

A fruit basket would have been nice, but instead we found that a flyer had been slipped under the door.

Dear Brainwashed Cowards,

You are nothing but puppets of the corrupt Shah. We will teach you a lesson you will never forget. Death to the Shah. Death to you.

My father crumpled the flyer and threw it away. "Let's find out where they're having the dinner buffet," he said.

The next day, half a dozen buses lined up in front of our hotel to take us to the lawn across from the White House. We were given Iranian flags and told to wave them at the Shah's arrival. Moments before we left, a man boarded our bus and introduced himself as a lawyer working for the Iranian government. "In case anybody attacks you," he told us, "please try to take his picture. This would be most useful."

We arrived at the White House to find a group of masked demonstrators carrying signs denouncing the Shah and his government. "Don't worry," my father assured me, "they're on the *other* side of the street."

Opposite the demonstrators, scaffolding had been built for the Shah's supporters. Speakers took turns giving speeches on the glories of Iran. To my delight, I found that the lawn had been strewn with miniature Iranian flags. "Help me find thirty of them," I asked my parents. "I'm going to hand them out in Miss Crocket's social studies class."

My mother and I headed toward the back of the lawn, while my father went to the front to look for more flags. A few minutes later, we heard my father say, "Look how many I found!" He held up his bounty. But his voice was drowned out by the twenty-one-gun salute announcing the arrival of the Shah's limousine. People started to cheer, but the cheering wasn't entirely cheerful. The demonstrators had crossed the road. They were stampeding toward us waving sticks with nails driven into them. People were screaming and running. Instead of Iranian flags, the lawn was suddenly covered with bloody and injured Iranians. My parents and I ran and ran and ran.

We found an empty bus and, not caring about its destination, climbed on board.

"I'm sorry, folks," the bus driver drawled, "y'all are gonna hafta get off this bus, 'cuz it's outta service and I'm on break."

Across the street, we found a police officer on horseback. "Excuse me," I said, "we're afraid we're going to get beaten up. Could you please help us get back to our hotel?"

Perhaps this officer had joined the police force because of the handsome uniforms or perhaps he wanted a job that let him ride a horse. He looked at us and said, "Sorry, that's not my job."

Spotting another bus, we boarded it immediately. "Do you have tickets?" the driver asked.

"How much are they?"

We paid twenty-one dollars and took our seats just as the bus started to leave. We had no idea where we were going. A recorded narration began.

"Our next stop is the Lincoln Memorial, built in honor of

Abraham Lincoln, the sixteenth president of the United States. On the north wall of this majestic memorial, you will see the words of the Gettysburg Address: 'Four score and seven years ago our fathers brought forth . . .' "

Three hours, four monuments, and one cab ride later, we arrived at our hotel. The lobby was filled with bandaged survivors exchanging horror stories. At the sight of all the wounded, my father turned to my mother and me and said, "Don't mention we went on a tour. It's going to look bad that we were having fun while everyone else was suffering." Before I could tell my father that the tour had *not* been fun, he was accosted by a friend, whose arm was now in a sling.

"Where have you three been the whole time? We were getting ready to call the hospitals."

"Well," my father sighed, "we had to walk back."

Like a story written in installments, a second flyer awaited us in our room.

Dear Brainwashed Cowards,
We are going to blow you up.

Even the prospect of the dinner buffet was no longer enough to keep us in the nation's capital. "That's it," my father announced. "We're leaving."

Six hours later, we found ourselves in the coach section of a crowded airplane, sitting in three different rows. We were thrilled to be headed home.

As the airplane took off, my father turned around and shouted from four rows ahead of me, "That really wasn't that bad. Firoozeh, you know how you like historical places? Well, we saw a bunch."

He continued, "Of course, I do have one regret."

"What's that?" I yelled back.

"I shouldn't have dropped all the flags. I'm sure I had enough for your whole class."

"That's okay," I replied. "We can always go back."

Î-raynians Need Not Apply

At the age of seventeen, my father began working for NIOC, the National Iranian Oil Company, as a student employee. He worked his way up the corporate ladder and eventually became a senior project manager. His lifetime of experience with oil refineries brought us to America, where he worked as a representative of NIOC, supervising American contractors in the design of an oil refinery in Isfahan. After thirty-three years of working with the same company, my father never doubted the security of his future.

But with the Iranian Revolution, my father's world turned upside down. The building of more refineries in Iran was halted and overnight my father's expertise was no longer needed. Although NIOC offered him other positions in Iran, none was within his field of interest. With much dismay, he requested and was reluctantly granted early retirement. My father was confident in his abilities to find a job in the United States.

Within a couple of weeks, he found an engineering position with an American company. As he was settling into his new job, a group of Americans in Tehran were taken hostage in the American embassy. My father was laid off.

Every evening, we sat in front of the television and watched the news for updates on the hostage situation. For 444 nights, we waited. With each passing day, palpable hatred grew among many Americans, hatred not just of the hostage takers but of all Iranians. The media didn't help. We opened our local paper one day to the screaming headline "Iranian Robs Grocery Store." Iran has as many fruits and nuts as the next country, but it seemed as if every lowlife who happened to be Iranian was now getting his fifteen minutes of fame.

Vendors started selling T-shirts and bumper stickers that said "Iranians Go Home" and "Wanted: Iranians, for Target Practice." Crimes against Iranians increased. People would hear my mother's thick accent and ask us, "Where are you from?" They weren't looking for a recipe for stuffed grape leaves. Many Iranians suddenly became Turkish, Russian, or French.

To add to my family's collective anxiety, my father's pension from Iran was cut off. The Iranian government told him that from now on, if he wanted his hard-earned retirement pay, he would have to go to Iran to collect it. Even worse, with the turmoil in Iran, the value of my father's pension dropped to the point of worthlessness.

At fifty-eight, my father found himself unemployed and with no prospects. Nobody wanted to hire an Iranian. My father returned to Iran to sell all our belongings. Within three weeks, he sold our house for a tenth of its previous value. A colleague bought our fourteen room-size Persian rugs for $1,300—and sold one of them for $15,000 a few months later.

Perhaps the greatest irony in the wave of Iranian-hating was that Iranians, as a group, are among the most educated and successful immigrants in this country. Our work ethic and obsession with education make us almost ideal citizens. Nobody asked our opinion of whether the hostages should be taken, and yet every single Iranian in America was paying the price. One kid throws a spitball and the whole class gets detention.

For my father to be treated like a second-class citizen truly stung. If there were ever a poster child for immigration, it would be Kazem. Perhaps nothing speaks louder than his obsession with voting.

When I became an American citizen, in college, my father called to ask whether I was planning to vote in the upcoming election. "If I have time," I answered. My father then told me that perhaps I did not deserve to be a citizen. Any immigrant who comes to this country and becomes a citizen and doesn't vote, according to him, should just go back.

"What about American citizens who are born here and don't vote?" I asked, egging him on.

"They need to be sent for six months to a nondemocratic country. Then they'll vote," he replied.

I told my father that his "Ship 'Em Abroad" program didn't sound too democratic to me, that perhaps included in the freedoms in this country is the freedom to be apathetic.

He hung up on me.

I voted.

But that wasn't the end of it. After every election, my father called me to ask me whom I had voted for. After several such phone calls, we realized that our votes simply negate each other. We stand on opposite sides of all issues. I have since learned not to share any information with my father, instead reminding him that the voting process is confidential, which explains why there are booths instead of, say, people just raising their hands in a public voting hall so that someone like my father can tell them they're wrong.

"Well," he always huffs, "you always vote for the wrong people anyway. Thank God for your mother."

My mother's voting ritual is a whole other story. She, like most Americans, doesn't fully comprehend the American political system. I'm convinced that the average American would have an easier time naming Elizabeth Taylor's ex-husbands than, say, his or her congressional leaders. To complicate matters, my mother does not understand English well enough to learn more, which is where my father comes in.

As soon as my father receives his voting pamphlet in the mail, he sits on the sofa, pen in hand, and reads it cover to cover. He underlines, he circles, he writes in the margins. If he doesn't know how to vote on an issue, he looks for an endorsement by firemen or police officers. In my father's world, firemen and police officers wear white cowboy hats. If the local firefighters' union thinks it's a good idea to raise taxes to build more tap dance studios, then so does my father.

Once my father decides how to vote on all the issues, he then practices democracy with a dash of dictatorship thrown in for good measure. He tells my mother how *she* should vote. My mother rarely questions my father's choices, and when she does, he answers her with one of his typical opinions: "Anybody with a brain can tell that's a no vote." (Chances are I voted yes.)

In 1980, however, despite my father's staunch devotion to freedom and fairness, he was still a foreigner with an accent, an accent that after the Iranian Revolution was associated with all things bad. He was treated like someone who should just pack up and go. But go where?

After selling our possessions in Iran, Kazem returned to America and started, yet again, looking for a job. Now, though, he no longer applied to American companies. He eventually applied for a job with a large oil company in Saudi Arabia. This entailed relocating, but we had no choice: by now, my parents had cut up all our credit cards, and our modest savings were disappearing quickly. After weeks of interviews and negotiations, he was offered an executive position and the contract was ready to sign. My father was hopeful for the first time since being laid off. Before signing the final papers, the lawyer asked for his passport, a requirement for any overseas job. At the sight of the Iranian passport, the lawyer turned pale and said, "I am so sorry, but the government of Saudi Arabia does not accept Iranians at this time. We thought you were an Arab."

My father resumed his job search. In *The Wall Street Journal*, he spotted an ad for an executive position with a Nigerian oil company. He immediately applied and was hired within two weeks. With its high salary and unlimited expansion potential, this job almost seemed too good to be true.

My father's first assignment was to go to New Jersey and negotiate the purchase of an oil refinery for $400 million. Once that was done, he was sent to Texas to purchase another refinery. He was thrilled to be using his expertise again.

After returning from his assignments, my father discovered that his first and only paycheck had bounced. He was told that there had been a small delay with funds being wired from Nigeria and that his second paycheck would cover the first. He had no option but to keep working.

A few days later, he came to the office to discover a swarm of journalists looking for information on a hot new breaking story. Apparently, the owner of the company was a con man who had already been deported from the United States once but had returned under an assumed name. My father packed his office supplies and left.

The hostages were finally freed. Besides them and their families, no one was happier than the Iranians living in America.

Shortly after their release, my father found a job with an American company, working as a senior engineer. His salary was half what it had been before the revolution, but he was nonetheless extremely grateful to wake up and go to work every day.

Throughout his job ordeal, my father never complained. He remained an Iranian who loved his native country but who also believed in American ideals. He only said how sad it was that people so easily hate an entire population simply because of the actions of a few. And what a waste it is to hate, he always said. What a waste.

Girls Just Wanna Have Funds

With the Iranian Revolution and my family's financial upheaval in the background, I had entered adolescence. At an age when most of my classmates were discovering the Nordstrom shoe department, I had watched my parents cut up their credit cards. Being unfashionable didn't bother me, but I was afraid I couldn't afford to go to college. I needed some funds.

Job prospects for fourteen-year-olds have never been rosy, so I settled on the old standby, baby-sitting. At a dollar per hour, I soon discovered, this was not going to get me anywhere. Some of my luckier friends baby-sat for families who rounded up to the nearest hour or threw in an extra two dollars for good measure. I always ended up with people who, after arriving home at midnight on a Saturday night, would spend fifteen minutes calculating exactly how much they owed me. "Five hours and twelve minutes, so that's five dollars and . . . twelve divided by sixty, that's about twenty cents, or is that thirty? Hold on, I need a piece of paper . . ."

After having baby-sat for every frugal family in town, I eventually hit the mother lode. My high school French teacher told me of a newly transplanted Parisian family that was looking for a French-speaking baby-sitter. Even though my French at the time was limited to asking whether Jacques was at the pool with Anne, I volunteered. I was told that the family had only one child, an eight-year-old daughter, and that they lived in Big Canyon, a gated community full of rich people.

I arrived with high hopes and a French dictionary. After giving me a tour of their large house, including the twenty-foot Buddha in the living room, the father asked me whether five dollars an hour would be sufficient. These people had clearly not researched the going rate for baby-sitters, and if the twenty-foot Buddha had not enlightened them, I was not about to start.

No diapers, no cooking, just one eight-year-old who would probably go to bed easily and five dollars per hour. This was too good to be true, but I knew it was true because if anyone deserved a break, it was I.

As soon as the parents left, the daughter plunked herself next to me on the posh leather sofa and immediately started hugging me and stroking my hair. I didn't want to get on her bad side early on in this lucrative job so I smiled as I tried to untangle her arms. The more I tried to extricate myself, the harder she clung. I had no idea the French were so affectionate.

I'd been wrestling with the child for half an hour when the lights in the living room went out automatically and the glass cabinets along the walls lit up from underneath, illuminating an extensive collection of Buddhas. I felt like King Tut, except that I was alive and trapped in the mausoleum with a deranged koala. No matter what I did, I could not get the kid off me. She refused to go to bed. She refused to eat dinner. She refused to budge. With thirty Buddhas watching me, I was suddenly enlightened as to why these people were so generous with the baby-sitter.

When the parents arrived three hours later, they found their daughter snoring on the sofa. She had finally fallen asleep and I had not dared move her, lest she wake up. Normally, parents might be upset by this, but not these people. God knows they were probably relieved to have gotten away from their daughter for a few hours. The father handed me a twenty-dollar bill and asked whether I was available the following night. I didn't know how to say in French "Not for all the tea in China would I return to this freak zone," so I just told him I had to study for a test.

My three traumatic hours of baby-sitting the Cling-on convinced me to retire from the field. I decided to switch to house-sitting, a far easier yet potentially lucrative line of work. I let all my friends and neighbors know that not only was I available during all vacations but I was also good with plants. The latter wasn't exactly true, since I didn't own any plants and had never actually taken care of any, but I figured if the soil is dry, I water.

My first job consisted of watering the indoor plants belonging to a family a couple of streets away from us. Monday morning, before school, I rode my bike to their house and started watering every plant, just as I had been instructed. All of a sudden, I heard music coming from one of the bedrooms upstairs. I froze. I stood in the kitchen, watering can in hand, unable to scream or move. After a few minutes, I put down the watering can, slowly tiptoed out of the kitchen, and ran out the front door. I could barely ride my bike home with my entire body trembling.

My father was in Iran trying to sell our house and I knew my mother would be of no help. I thought about calling the police, but how would I know whether anything had been stolen? Plus, I didn't know how to reach the family, so I decided to do nothing. After a few days, I imagined all their plants dead. Overcome with guilt, I decided to risk my life and enter the house again. Grabbing our fireplace poker, I rode my bike to their house. As I opened the front door, I yelled, "DAD, KEEP THE DOG OUT. I DON'T WANT HIM TO BITE ANYONE. YOU KNOW HOW MEAN HE IS."

I ran in the house and dumped water on all the plants as fast as I could, even the ones that I had been instructed to "gently mist." I continued my conversation with my imaginary dad. "HOLD ON TO HIS LEASH!" I screamed.

When the family returned a few days later, I told them they wouldn't have to pay me: I had come to the house only twice, because there might have been a robber in the house the previous Monday, listening to music in an upstairs bedroom.

"What time were you here?" the wife asked.

"Seven-fifteen in the morning," I told her.

"You heard the clock radio," she informed me.

She paid me in full but never asked me to house-sit again.

Shortly thereafter, another family asked me to take care of their indoor cats for ten days. Except for the goldfish we bought every year for the Persian New Year I had never owned a pet, but I accepted the job.

These people had four cats, Ketchup, Mustard, Relish, and Mayo. I should have known better than to get involved with people who would name their cats after condiments, but common sense is an acquired trait.

My first day on the job, I rode my bike to their house and did everything as I'd been told. I emptied the litter box, opened up the stinking cans of cat food, gave the cats two scoops of dried food, and filled up their water bowls. I didn't really play with the cats, because like most houses overrun with indoor cats, this one was no treat for the senses. As I was leaving, I noticed that the door to the patio was wide open. I shut and locked it.

I returned the next morning to repeat my routine. The cats were meowing considerably more than the day before, but I figured they were hungry.

The next day, they were meowing loudly and screeching intermittently.

The following day, their intermittent screeches were peppered with leaps across the furniture.

I thought that perhaps if I played with them, they might calm down a bit. The problem was that whenever I went near one of them, it would arch its body and snarl. My goldfish had never done that, but I was nonetheless able to understand the international symbol for "I'm going to scratch out your eyeballs."

By the tenth day, these frisky felines spent all their time running around the house in endless circles, screeching and scratching. I chalked up their strange behavior to the absence of their beloved owners.

That night the owners called. "Why did you close the patio door?" the mother screamed at me.

"I closed it because it was open," I replied.

"How did you expect the cats to get any exercise?" she screamed back.

"But I thought they were indoor cats," I told her.

"The patio is their play area. Didn't you notice their behavior? You have mentally damaged my cats!"

"You don't have to pay me," I told her.

She paid me, but she never asked me to house-sit again.

My next job came courtesy of my friend Chris, who informed me that one of her very wealthy neighbors, who happened to be the mother of a very famous clothing designer, was looking for someone to clean her silverware. This job paid six dollars per hour. Chris also told me that this woman, whom I will call Mrs. Cheapo to protect her anonymity, had estimated that this was at least a twenty-dollar job.

I rode my bike to her house, arriving promptly at eight on a sunny Saturday morning. Mrs. Cheapo led me to her dining room table, where she had a heap of silverware stacked three feet high. Judging by the black tarnish, people were still traveling by horse and buggy the last time these pieces were cleaned. She handed me a foul-smelling cream and a couple of washcloths.

"Do you have a pair of latex gloves I could borrow?" I asked her.

"No, the polish might ruin them."

If my life were a movie script written by someone more intelligent than I, I would have gotten up and gone home, but not before pausing long enough to tell her that her daughter's designs were frumpy. In the real-life version, I got up and told her I had to go home to get a pair of gloves.

I rode my bike home feverishly and returned with my mother's dishwashing gloves. I set to work. Without taking a break, I scrubbed intensely, trying my best not to inhale the noxious fumes. I cleaned every nook and cranny of every fork, spoon, knife, butter knife, cheese server, iced-tea spoon, carving knife, and oyster fork, not to mention the pieces whose function completely eluded me. I sorted all the pieces in matching piles and informed her that I was done.

"I can't believe you're finished!" she squealed, staring at the shiny piles. I was used to hearing that from my teachers at school, but I assumed this declaration of surprise would translate into a fat tip.

"Well," said Mrs. Cheapo, taking out a wad of cash, "let's see, you were here for one hour and twenty minutes, so here's eight dollars."

"But I thought this was a twenty-dollar job," I reminded her.

"Not with you, honey," she said. "It didn't take you that long."

I should have hurled a few oyster forks at her, but instead I thanked her and rode my bike home. She was right about one thing. The polish did ruin the gloves.

Through my friend Marilyn, I found out that the local movie theater was looking for summer help. I was hired to work at the concession stand, where I was responsible for selling the type of food that should come with a free angiogram.

The popcorn came in four sizes, small, medium, large, and jumbo. During the entire summer, only three people ordered the small popcorn. They were European and had apparently come to watch the movie. Most patrons ordered the jumbo popcorn, a snack whose container could double as an infant bathtub. The instructions were always the same: "Please put butter in the bottom, middle, and top. No dry spots." Not even when my relatives ended their fasts during the holy month of Ramadan had I seen people consume this much food.

The lobby of the movie theater was plastered with signs declaring OUR POPCORN IS MADE WITH REAL BUTTER. Judging by our brisk popcorn sales, I suggested to my manager that perhaps a similar advertising campaign might improve hot dog sales. "Our hot dogs are made with REAL innards." Just like Galileo's, my ideas were rejected.

The most popular drink that summer was Tab, a diet soda that tasted like liquid tin. Unfortunately, our Tab machine was always broken and we offered no other diet drinks. After placing an order for the jumbo popcorn with extra butter, most people asked for a large Tab. This is when things got ugly. "What?" they would always scream at me. "It's *broken?*" Then they'd ask to see the manager, as if through sheer assertiveness they could get the machine fixed. I always had the urge to enlighten them: "Look, you're about to consume ten thousand calories of fat, so a diet drink isn't going to make a difference. In fact, may I suggest some innards?"

My summer at the movie theater taught me one thing: I had to look for a better-paying job, preferably one that did not involve selling Jujubes. A string of jobs followed, but none ever paid well. My efforts at amassing funds were not hugely successful.

Watching me trying to save money, my father repeatedly told me how bad he felt at being unable to help with my college tuition. He spent his days lamenting his inability to foresee the revolution and the ensuing economic collapse. "I should've sold everything and brought the money to America a long time ago" became his mantra.

As college approached, I stumbled upon a talent better than selling popcorn or polishing silver. I started writing scholarship essays. I wrote essay after essay about my life and my dreams and my goals. I wrote about volunteering as a clown in a children's hospital. I wrote about being my mother's interpreter. I wrote that ever since I was a little girl, I had wanted to go to college. And I wrote that my aunt Sedigeh should have been able to go to college but instead had to get married when she was fourteen.

And the funds just flowed in.

Joyeuse Noëlle

One Saturday morning during my junior year of high school, I showed up at the University of California at Irvine to compete in an impromptu speech contest sponsored by the Alliance Française, a French language school. I, along with a few dozen college and high school students, was given one hour to prepare a speech in French entitled "Responsibility Toward Technology." The first prize was two months at the Alliance Française in Paris.

I had been taking French since seventh grade, and under the tutelage of my high school teacher, Mr. Polkingharn, affectionately known as Le Polk, I had become quite fluent. My fellow high school students often asked me how I had managed to learn the language so quickly. I always told them that it had something to do with my inability to do a cartwheel, shoot a basket, or roller-skate. God had to compensate somehow.

To qualify for the contest, all participants had to sign a statement saying that they had never spent more than two weeks in a French-speaking country and that neither parent was a native speaker. My parents' French was limited to a handful of words that had crept into Persian, including *minijupe* (miniskirt), *bigoudi* (hair roller), *abat-jour* (lampshade), and *coup d'état*. The French word most commonly used in Iran was *chic*, a word that accurately described what we were not.

The only language heard in our house besides Persian was Shushtari, a version of Old Persian spoken by my father and his family, whose ancestors came from the historic city of Shushtar, in southern Iran. About 1,750 years ago, King Shapur I led the Persians in a fight against the Roman emperor Valerian. After winning the battle, the Persians brought the captured Roman engineers to Shushtar to design dams, water mills, artificial canals, and an irrigation system, many of which still work today. If Walt Disney had ever seen Shushtar, he would have created Ancientland to be nestled alongside Frontierland and Fantasyland.

The language of Shushtari, with its abundance of animal and plant imagery, reflects the simple agricultural life of its residents. Many words exist in Shushtari that do not exist in Persian. For instance, the word *peshkel* means animal droppings that are round, like a goat's or sheep's. When two people look alike, my aunt Sedigeh describes them as being "like two halves of a *peshkel*." And to reveal what is truly valuable in life, my aunt Fatimeh always uses the Shushtari proverb "Any gift from a true friend is valuable, even if it's a hollow walnut shell."

It's fair to say that the Shushtari floating in my house did not give me any edge in the French language. It did, however, teach me that people sometimes talk louder and laugh harder in their native tongue, as evidenced by my father and his siblings. It also trained my ear for accents and thus eventually got me into trouble.

Even though I was the youngest contestant in the impromptu-speech contest, I placed first. Unbeknownst to me, this was met with suspicion. Apparently, some people thought that my Parisian accent was too authentic for a foreigner. Perhaps taking their cue from Detective Clouseau, a couple of the judges decided to do a little investigative work.

After the contest, my parents started receiving phone calls in French. They became a somewhat regular, though inexplicable, part of our lives; the phone would ring, and then my father or mother would say, "Vait, vait, pehleeze . . . *Firoozeh*." I would pick up the receiver to find somebody from the Alliance Française with a piddling question or comment.

"I would like to verify the spelling of your last name."

"I would like to congratulate you personally."

"Have you read anything by Camus? He's quite good."

These French phone calls made my already nervous parents even more anxious. "Why do they keep speaking French with us if they know we don't speak the language?" they always asked me. I had no clue. I just assumed they were forgetful. My mother finally reached her own conclusion. "Nobody understands their English," concluded my mother. "And they know that."

Two weeks after my seventeenth birthday, I was on an airplane bound for Paris. I was scheduled to arrive two days before the national celebration of the French Revolution, Bastille Day. I had never been so excited in my entire life. I couldn't wait to meet my host family. I couldn't wait to eat an authentic baguette. I couldn't wait to make French friends. This was going to be the best summer of my entire life, the kind of summer that somebody would want to make a movie out of. And as soon as I set foot in the Paris airport, I was whisked away by two gendarmes.

I had no idea that traveling with an Iranian passport would

qualify me for special treatment. These men found it odd that three years after the revolution, a seventeen-year-old Iranian should be traveling by herself and staying in Paris for two months. In a small, windowless room, I explained to them in French, but with a perky Southern California demeanor, all about the contest and how I had won and how much I was looking forward to seeing the Louvre and going to cafés and eating a crepe on a street corner.

"You don't know anybody in Paris?" they asked me.

"Did anyone give you any materials to distribute?"

"How is it that you speak French so well if you are only a student of French?"

"Do you plan on returning to America afterward?"

These people clearly thought my life was a lot more exciting that it was. After answering all their questions, I had to endure the luggage search. My suitcase, roughly the size of a coffin, was on loan from Aunt Sedigeh. It had previously been used to transport two large Persian rugs and an entire samovar set from Iran.

The gendarmes started sifting through the clothes and the myriad of gifts I had brought for my host family. When they reached the stuffed Minnie Mouse, they decided they had had enough. They zipped up my suitcase and politely wished me a nice stay.

After my rendezvous with the welcoming committee, I searched the airport for someone carrying a sign with my name on it. Once I found her, I was greeted with "Where have you been?" I explained to her that I was a VIP, a Very Iranian Person, and things just take longer for us.

Before coming to Paris, I had corresponded once with my host family, mainly to find out what kinds of gifts to bring. Michel and Christiane were journalists working for *Libération*, a left-leaning newspaper. They also had a six-month-old daughter. I had envisioned myself spending evenings having enlightening discussions over home-cooked French meals. "Pass the béarnaise sauce, please—and tell me again, Michel, what you really think of the ramifications of industrialism in nineteenth-century France."

Upon arriving, I gave them the gifts: the coffee-table book on California, the signed limited-edition print of the Ferris wheel on Balboa Island, the T-shirts from Newport Beach, the homemade chocolate chip cookies, the homemade baklava, and the large Minnie Mouse. Once my hosts had opened all the presents, Christiane blithely informed me that the next morning they would be leaving for the countryside, where they would be staying for the entire summer, but here were the keys to the apartment. She also told me the location of the nearest twenty-four-hour market. I then did what any self-respecting person would do: I asked to go with them. "*Non,*" replied Christiane.

It became painfully obvious to me that there was to be no cultural exchange with these people. The only exchange they were interested in was the exchange of currency between them and the rental office.

Michel and Christiane's small apartment on the rue de Turbigo was filled with books and magazines. Bookshelves lined every room. From Japanese art to Russian literature to the works of Dante and Joyce, every topic was covered—except of course, hospitality. Had I not met Michel and Christiane but simply stayed in their apartment, I probably would have liked them.

The tiny bathroom came with a three-year stack of *Zoom,* a photography magazine that prominently featured breasts in every pictorial, but in an intellectual way. For a spread on the disappearing tribes of Africa, the locals were featured alongside a lineup of topless Caucasian models wearing African masks. What better way to showcase the wildflowers of Provence than by painting a few topless models purple and placing them among the flowers? Even the ads followed the same theme. In a coffee ad, a dark-skinned model was featured sitting on a hill of beans. Both the beans and the model were naked.

During my years as a French student, every textbook I had ever read had elaborated upon the unforgettable jubilance known as Bastille Day, the parade down the Champs-Elysées, the fireworks, the general merriment, and the cherished memories born only of this event. Sitting alone in the apartment the day after my arrival, I realized that I was going to be spending this momentous holiday by myself in a tiny apartment far away from the festivities. Since I knew nobody in Paris, I decided to go talk to the concierge to see if she had any ideas.

According to my books on French culture, concierges were usually old ladies living alone on the ground floor of apartment buildings. They were usually pictured peeking from behind their lace curtains to see the comings and goings of the apartment dwellers. One is supposed to consult the concierge about the mail or a lost key, never for social advice. But I was desperate.

I knocked on the door and was pleasantly surprised to be greeted by Noëlle, a plump, jovial woman in her early forties. I explained to her that I had just arrived in Paris from California and was looking for something to do on Bastille Day. The minute she heard the word "California," she perked up even more. "*Une californienne!*" she exclaimed. I didn't really want to disappoint her by pointing out that I was actually *une iranienne,* so I just smiled. She wanted to know whether I lived near Hollywood and whether I knew any famous people. I explained to her that I lived an hour away from Hollywood; as for famous people, I thought of telling her that my father is directly descended from

the Prophet Muhammad, but I knew that wasn't the kind of famous person she was inquiring about.

Noëlle told me to meet her the following night so we could go
to the Champs-Elysées together. She said she couldn't wait. Neither could I.

The next evening, I put on a Hawaiian shirt, jeans, and the
spanking-new Adidas sneakers I had bought for my trip. I
knocked on Noëlle's door, but the woman who answered bore
no resemblance to the concierge I had met the night before.

Noëlle was clad in a body-hugging red knit dress that accentu-
ated her ample curves. The plunging neckline barely covered her
enormous chest. With each breath she took, I expected her bosom
to just break free and come out to watch the parade with us.

We started walking the three blocks to the Métro station,
catching the attention of every creepy male in the City of Lights.
As Noëlle jiggled and wiggled down the street, I thought of just
skipping the parade since we had managed to start our own.

During the long Métro ride, we sat surrounded by the kind
of men I always associate with windowless vans bearing
bumper stickers that say IF THIS VAN'S A-ROCKIN', DON'T COME
A-KNOCKIN'. Unlike me, Noëlle was completely enamored of
the attention, although, to her credit, she never talked to any of
the men. She was too busy inquiring about California and specif-
ically, California men. In search of a husband, she told me, she
had recently moved to Paris from the countryside, but she was
hugely disappointed with the men: according to her, they were
all married. I was surprised that she had any minimum standards,
since her dress and high heels gave the impression that anyone
in possession of a simple set of one X and one Y chromosome
would suffice.

We reached the Champs-Elysées approximately ten minutes

after the rest of the population of Western Europe. Noëlle and I moved around trying to find a good spot, but no matter where we went, all we could see was the backs of people's heads. I didn't think anything could be worse than the after-Christmas sale at Nordstrom, but I was clearly wrong.

The parade started and ended. I saw nothing.

Once the festivities were over, Noëlle and I made our way to the Métro station, only to find that the same fourteen rows of people who had been ahead of us at the parade were now ahead of us in line for the train. "*Pas de problème,*" chirped Noëlle. "*Nous chercherons un taxi.*" The idea of looking for a taxi was a fine one, except that apparently all the drivers had taken the night off—they had probably been standing in front of us at the parade. After walking half a dozen blocks, Noëlle suggested that we just walk the rest of the way home. It was one A.M.

Normally, I cannot stay awake past ten o'clock. My goal throughout high school was to stay up long enough to watch *Saturday Night Live*. I never made it. In college, my parents had no need to worry about my getting involved with drugs and alcohol, since by the time most parties started, I was in my third cycle of REM sleep.

I am also legendary among my friends for my complete lack of a sense of direction, making me the perfect kidnap victim, no blindfold necessary. Drive me anywhere and I will be unable to find my way back. It was therefore a great irony that I found myself in a foreign city trying to make my way home *way* past my bedtime.

I spent the entire walk home making deals with God: "If you just get me home, I will never ask for anything again." Between conversations with the Almighty, I listened for the *click-click* of Noëlle's heels, a Morse code of sorts, to guide me back to the rue de Turbigo. By then, we had run out of conversation, or rather, Noëlle had nothing more to say about men. Much to her disappointment, I didn't have much to contribute on the topic since I was, to put it kindly, a late bloomer.

School started a few days later. The classes, like the Bastille Day parade, were a huge disappointment. All my teachers were in their early twenties and none seemed very interested in teaching. Perhaps they resented being stuck in Paris during the summer, a season when the French normally evacuate the capital. One teacher spent the whole time flirting with the men in class while completely ignoring the women. Another made us translate the lyrics of the works of Jacques Brel, a famous performer whose songs would have been appropriate for *Suicide: The Musical*. We spent hours plodding through the songs, while our teacher sat with a far-off look in her eyes. My English versions did not do them justice, but then again, the teacher had a certain hands-off style of teaching, a style that translated into her sitting in the corner recalling, perhaps, a summer spent elsewhere. She helped us only reluctantly, as when none of our dictionaries had the word *putain*, slang for "prostitute." With apologies to Monsieur Brel, the song "Jef":

No Jef, you're not alone
Stop crying like that in front of everyone
Because a fake blonde dumped you yet again
No Jef, you're not alone
But I'm ashamed to see you cry shamelessly in front of everybody
Because a three-quarter whore popped out of your life

Then we moved on to "Fernand," a funerary march.

To think that Fernand is dead
To think that Fernand has died
To think that I'm the only one behind
To think that he's the only one in front
Him in his last beer
Me in my fog
Him in his hearse
Me in my desert

By the end of that song, we were able to conjugate the verb "to die" in every tense.

Had I made some friends during my melancholic French lessons, I would have at least been a few degrees happier than Jef or Fernand. Unfortunately, the students in my classes were quite a bit older than I was and most were newly arrived immigrants struggling to learn French. These were not people hoping to find Gertrude Stein's favorite haunt; they were hoping to find a job. The few interesting people I did meet were leaving in three days to go somewhere else. No one, except for the people selling key chains under the Eiffel Tower, actually stayed in Paris during the summer.

The upside of my lonely two months was that I became completely fluent in French. Having loads of free time, I also managed to see just about every museum in the city. Whatever culture I lacked after having spent six years in Southern California, I more than made up for.

The downside of my summer was realizing that maybe the joys of being seventeen, even in Paris, were highly exaggerated. I wondered if the summer somehow foreshadowed the rest of my life. Maybe I was doomed to a really lonely existence where the

only pleasure came not from human company but from crois-
sants. Maybe someday I would end up thinking Jacques Brel's
lyrics *were* uplifting.

A few months after my return to California, I received a letter
from Noëlle letting me know that she had moved to New Cale-
donia, where, according to her, the ratio of men to women was
five to one. I remembered her kindness in taking me to the
Champs-Elysées on Bastille Day to fulfill one of my dreams.
Granted, she had mistaken me for a real Californian, someone
who perhaps knew Paul Newman or Cher. But in exchange for
making one of my dreams come true, I sincerely hoped that she
would find Monsieur Merveilleux waiting for her on that little island in the Pacific.

If someone were to make a movie of my summer in Paris, it
would not be the touching coming-of-age film I had hoped for,
but rather a black-and-white filled with close-ups of furrowed
brows and croissant crumbs. There would be no theme song, just
the sound of the Métro doors opening and closing and opening
and closing. Against this backdrop of teenage angst, there would
have to be a symbol, a representation of the confidence that
comes with eventual intellectual and spiritual growth. This
would, *bien sûr,* be most effectively depicted by a judicious scat-
tering of topless models in the background.

The Wedding

My marriage started out with a big, fat lie:

I told my parents that François's family was happy about our engagement.

I had to. In the Iranian culture, fathers will consent to a marriage only if the future groom and his family worship the bride. There is no getting around this detail. If there is any problem with the groom's family, forget it. Engagement off. Moving on to the next suitor.

When I first started dating François, his mother declared that I "would never be allowed to set foot in her house." This was *before* she met me.

Before meeting me, François had a longtime French girlfriend. From all accounts, she was an intelligent and capable person. But she was Jewish. Her religion was a problem until François started dating me. Compared to a Muslim, the Jewish girlfriend didn't seem so bad after all. I once asked François if there was anybody he could have dated that would have bothered his mother more. "Well," he said, "a black Communist bisexual would have *really* irked her."

My parents had a completely different reaction to François. They first heard of him during the summer after my junior year in college, six months after we had met. For five and half of those months, François and I had known we were going to get married, but had not said anything to our parents. I had simply informed my parents that I was dating somebody and I wanted them to meet him.

Dating, like the rodeo circuit or trout farming, is a completely foreign concept to my parents. They, like all their sisters and brothers, never dated, their marriages having been arranged by family members. My mother learned what she knows about dating from *Days of Our Lives*, especially Hope and Bo's tumultuous relationship. The only dates my father knew about contained pits.

The first time they met François, my parents insisted on taking him to the nicest Persian restaurant in Los Angeles. My father ordered the appetizer sampler, which François ate with gusto while questioning my mother about the ingredients:

"Is this spice sumac?"

"Are these the thin-skinned Persian cucumbers?"

"Is the feta made with sheep's milk?"

Once the appetizers were finished, François selected the most copious dish on the menu, the *sultani*, a combination of lamb, beef, and chicken kebob on an enormous mound of rice. His order arrived, looking as though someone had just grilled an entire petting zoo. François ate and ate and ate. My father asked me, in Persian, whether he always ate like this. My mother said, in Persian, that she hoped he wasn't going to get sick. Meanwhile, François kept eating.

By the time he was done, there was not a grain of rice left on his large oval plate. My mother told him how lucky he was that he could eat enough food for three people and not be fat. François was of normal weight—although he did outweigh me, which fulfilled one of my two requirements for dating a guy. The other requirement was a total lack of interest in watching sports on television. François fulfilled that one, too.

Unbelievably, he ordered dessert, exclaiming that he couldn't possibly imagine skipping the rose water and pistachio ice cream. By then, I was just hoping that if he did throw up, it wouldn't happen in my father's car.

Once we arrived at my house, I asked François why he had eaten so much. "I know that Middle Easterners love to feed people and I wanted to make a good impression on your parents," he said. "But I need to go lie down now."

My parents did like François, not because of his appetite for Persian food, but because he was kind. And because I was in love with him.

My mother had always hoped that I would marry an Iranian doctor, someone whom she could speak to without an interpreter, a man whose parents would consider me the best thing that had ever happened to their son. She had held steadfastly to her dream, thinking that as soon as I reached my late teens, I would become the Iranian daughter whom she could relate to, the daughter who would dutifully let her parents help her select a mate.

Ever since we came to America, I had regarded my mother as a mere source of entertainment. This was a woman whose English required translation into English, a woman who listed the Gourdins in her phone book under "N" for "Neighbor" but who listed her hairdresser, Patricia, under "A" so her number would be on the first page. She had attended one PTA meeting during my entire educational career and had not understood a single word. Whenever I was required to bring a snack for some club meeting, my mother always wanted to make feta cheese and basil rolled in flat bread, or *sholeh zard,* a neon-yellow dessert made with saffron. "Forget it," I always told her, wishing she could just figure out how to make oatmeal raisin cookies. My mother was, in American adolescent vernacular, out of it.

Perhaps the people we think we know best are the ones who surprise us most. Once my mother realized that I wanted to marry François, she said, "He will be like a third son to me," and wiped the tears off her face. At that very moment, my mother threw aside everything she and her generation knew about marriage and entered a new world where daughters select their own husbands. She became a pioneer.

My father was just happy that I was getting married. Having only one daughter, he was particularly pleased that François asked his permission to marry me. François later told me that while delivering his Please-take-good-care-of-my-daughter speech, my father kept trying on my engagement ring on his own finger. "I just made sure he knew I wasn't proposing to him," François reported.

As soon as our wedding plans became official, we started making the guest list. Despite initial misgivings, François's parents decided to attend.

François's Sister No. 2 also agreed to come to the wedding. His maternal grandmother, whom he adored and considered to be his biggest influence, decided not to attend. François's oldest sister declined to come, stating that there was no way she would be in the same room as her mother or Sister No. 2. Brother-in-law No. 1, whom François had known since the age of seven, declined to come, stating that, having been virtually disinherited by his in-laws, he could not possibly attend. Brother-in-law No. 2 declined to come, probably because there just isn't enough

Mylanta in the world. François's only maternal aunt was not invited because she and my mother-in-law had fought over some land in Greece twenty years ago and were not on speaking terms. None of his four maternal cousins was invited, and I never asked why. I doubt they would have attended anyway. His paternal aunt and uncle declined to attend, as did their adult children. François's paternal grandmother did decide to attend, enlarging François's side of the wedding party to a whopping four family members.

In contrast to François's family, mine were busy making plans for a joyous occasion. My parents, like Santa Claus, were faced with a long list of names. This was the first wedding among my siblings, and my parents could not possibly fathom leaving anybody out. The reception hall had a maximum capacity of 165, which is a problem when just the aunts, uncles, cousins, and second cousins add up to 98 people. My parents agonized over the guest list, recalling every one of their friends back in Abadan. "We can't possibly leave *them* out" became a regular refrain. I didn't know half the people on the list. "Who are the Abbasis and why are we inviting them?" I wanted to know. "They invited us to their daughter's wedding last year. Plus, they live in Australia. They won't come." They came, and they brought a niece with them.

On a dozen occasions, invitations addressed to "Mr. and Mrs." came back announcing that six would be attending. Since our wedding was taking place in the summer, our guests who themselves had houseguests decided to just bring them along. We invited 140 people, 163 accepted; 181 showed up.

François and I had agreed that we would be married both in the Catholic Church and in a traditional Persian ceremony. The tough part was finding a Catholic priest who would be willing to officiate at a mixed marriage. François called several churches but was told that he would have to go to the church where he was a member. François had attended church a handful of times in his entire life. He was as Catholic as I was Muslim.

I decided to try contacting the Catholic church in my neighborhood in Newport Beach. I called and told the priest that my future husband was French but we hoped to get married in Southern California, where my family lived. I told him that of course I had never attended church because I was Muslim, but if I were Catholic, I would have attended his church, since it was my neighborhood Catholic church. "Well . . . " he said.

I continued: "I'm a very decent person. I could be Catholic, Jewish, you name it. All religions basically say the same thing and I would just fit right in in any of them."

"Well, that's not exactly—" he said.

"What I mean is that they all work toward the same goal," I interrupted.

Maybe he knew no other way to end the conversation, but the priest agreed to meet with me.

Father Christopher turned out to be a kind and enlightened man with a wonderful sense of humor. He agreed to marry us, although our wedding would not include the communion—it was sort of a Catholic ceremony lite. We had to meet with him a dozen times to discuss married life and religion. We also had to attend a retreat, held at a convent, which was aimed at preparing us for the challenges of marriage. On the first day, one of the speakers mentioned a seminar about the "unique challenges faced by mixed marriages." I attended, but found out that the "mixed marriages" he referred to did not involve Jews or Muslims, but rather Protestants, Orthodox Christians, and others who still believe in Jesus Christ, but with a different set of details.

Planning the Persian ceremony, or *aqd*, was by far the simplest part of our wedding. Ever since immigrating to America, my aunt Sedigeh and uncle Abdullah had earned a living by translating official documents and serving as notary publics. Uncle Abdullah also officiated at *aqd* ceremonies, a job that allowed him to utilize his in-depth knowledge of Arabic and the Koran. More important, this job meant that Aunt Sedigeh had the scoop on every impending marriage for miles around.

The *aqd* ceremony is traditionally held at the bride's house and is limited to family members and close friends. Our guests also included my second-grade teacher, Mrs. Sandberg. Since my parents' condominium was too small, my uncle Ali and aunt Linda kindly allowed us the use of their house. This was a fitting choice, because Uncle Ali was the first person in my family to marry a non-Iranian. He had met Linda, a blond nurse, when he was a medical resident in America. Initially, there was much concern about his choice. Although none of us had ever met Linda, obviously she did not know how to make Persian food. What would become of my uncle Ali? Could an Iranian man survive life without basmati rice and lamb stew?

Not only did Linda become a fabulous Persian cook, she also learned Italian cooking and became the quintessential hostess. She accomplished this while being employed full-time helping Ali run his medical practice. Now the family wonders what my uncle would have ever done without her. "He got lucky," they all agree.

In preparing for the *aqd*, we needed a *sofreh*, which is traditionally a hand-sewn cloth, roughly the size of a queen-size bedspread, on which the family arranges foods and objects, all of which hold special meaning.

At the head of the *sofreh* are the mirror and candleholders, symbolizing purity and love. Iranian families pass these objects from generation to generation. My father, the hopeless romantic, sold theirs after they were married. This was shortly before he decided to sell my mother's wedding band so they could stay at the Caspian Sea for an extra week.

We ended up renting the *sofreh*, the mirror, and the candleholders from an Iranian woman who does a brisk business providing the apparatus for *aqd* ceremonies. For many Iranians, moving to America meant having to leave the large mirror and candelabrum set back home. Thus, a unique rental business was born.

The *sofreh* also holds an assortment of sweets—sugar-coated almonds, baklava, almond cookies, and rice cookies. All the sweets were prepared by Aunt Dordooneh, who is technically not my aunt. She is my cousin Morteza's wife's aunt, but she has baked her way into everybody's heart, including my husband's, who also calls her *khaleh*, "aunt." The week before my wedding, she showed up at our house every day and held marathon baking sessions, filling our house with the aroma of rose water, butter, and roasted nuts.

In addition to the sweets, there was also a basket of almonds and walnuts, representing fertility, and a bowl of honey, for a sweet life. A platter of feta cheese and herbs and flat bread represented happiness and prosperity. Finally, we had a small wooden tree with carved radishes placed on the tip of each branch, which didn't represent anything but looked cute.

The ceremony began with François and me sitting facing the mirror with everybody crowding around the *sofreh* trying to get a good view. Uncle Abdullah began his speech in Persian, read passages from the Koran in Arabic, then translated everything into English. While he was doing his part, several aunts and female cousins held a small cloth over our heads and rubbed two sugar loaves together. This is supposed to ensure the raining of happiness into the couple's life.

When we were finally asked whether we wanted to marry each other, the groom is supposed to answer yes right away, but the bride is expected to take her sweet time and cause a little bit of last-minute anxiety for the groom and his family. When my uncle asked whether I wanted to marry François, I said nothing. My family yelled the traditional response: "She has gone to pick flowers." My uncle repeated his question. Again, I said nothing. The family yelled, "She has gone to bring rose water." My uncle asked a third time. This time, I said yes. Everyone cheered as my uncle declared us husband and wife.

When I call my parents at home, I usually speak to my mother first. When I ask to speak to my father, I often hear him yell in the background, "Tell her I've gone to pick flowers." If I happen to be in a hurry, I'll tell my mother to ask him to stop his nonsense and pick up the phone. Then I hear him say, "Tell her I've gone to get some rose water." He finds this very amusing.

After the *aqd* was over, everybody hugged and kissed, then hugged and kissed some more. This was followed by everybody taking pictures, and everybody crowding into everybody else's picture. The picture taking went on for a couple of hours, during which François complained that his face hurt from having to smile so much. "And," he added, "I've never been kissed by so many people in one day."

It's difficult to separate Iranians from their tradition of endlessly hugging and kissing on both cheeks. Women kiss women,

men kiss women, and big hairy men kiss other burly men. For-eigners, especially men, tend to find this tradition a bit discon-certing. Since the French also kiss twice on the cheek, François was not completely frightened by the throng of relatives waiting to give him a peck. He did, however, complain about certain relatives whose pecks were a little juicier than he would have liked. I've known Americans who, unaware of the kissing ritual, have wanted to run for the nearest exit at the sight of a pucker-ing Iranian uncle approaching with open arms. Even after my church ceremony, when everyone is supposed to leave the church quietly and in order, my relatives broke into a major kissing cere-mony, making us look as if we had never been to a church wed-ding before, which was true.

The most difficult part of my wedding was finding a location for the reception. Iranian weddings usually start at ten P.M. and end at two A.M. This eliminates all clubs and outdoor venues. Iranian food must be served. This eliminates all hotels, which make most of their money from their own catering. We had a small budget. This eliminated all locations with landscaping or English-speaking employees.

Our reception ended up in an Indian-Chinese restaurant near the airport. The business had started out as an Indian restaurant, but sales had been slow. Showing true immigrant tenacity, the owners added Chinese items as well. This was a place where one could order tandoori chicken or crab fu-yung, lentil soup or fish ball soup, and where the condiments included both soy sauce and chutney. The restaurant reminded me of a Pakistani rug shop I know in Northern California, which in addition to car-pets, started selling used computer parts and eventually added falafel. I assume, given a few years, leg waxing will also be a part of their repertoire.

The manager of the restaurant was a large Indian man with an overhanging stomach. The big tummy worked on Buddha but not on this guy. To add to his appeal, the whites of his eyes were the color of egg yolks and were further highlighted by being permanently bloodshot. This man could have easily been in *Star Wars*.

The night of my wedding, he stood in front of the locked door to the restaurant and said, "I will only let you in if you give me an extra four hundred dollars in cash right now." With the guests arriving in an hour, my father, who is significantly smaller than the manager, didn't have many options. Unfortunately, or perhaps fortunately, I did not hear about this until a few weeks after the fact. It's fair to say the bride's yelling and screaming would not have made for the most memorable wedding-day moment.

Our reception was a typical Iranian party with lots of music, too much makeup, and great food. As François and I entered, everyone stood up and cheered. We went around to each table, receiving more hugs, kisses, and wishes for a happy future. Aunt Sedigeh followed us, throwing tiny fake gold Persian coins over our heads. In ancient Persia, the gold would have been real. Everyone, even the busboys, knew the coins were fake. Everyone, that is, except for my new sister-in-law, who spent the evening feverishly collecting them.

When it came time to eat, we were the first ones in line, followed by Father Christopher. ("This is one reception I don't want to miss," he had told us.) The meal consisted of the traditional sweet carrot rice with almonds, saffron, and chicken; lima-bean rice with lamb shanks; eggplant stew; herb stew; stuffed grape leaves; and cucumber, tomato, and herb salad. My parents had also ordered an entire lamb to be roasted.

The Persians, like the Romans and Greeks before them, believe in slaughtering a lamb when something good happens. This is supposed to ward off the evil eye. Marriages, job offers, new cars, and new babies are always accompanied by this ancient ritual. In Iran, families who cannot afford a lamb use a chicken. Wealthier families usually donate the meat to the poor.

Iranians in America have had to tweak this tradition a bit. Slaughtering a lamb on one's front porch in Los Angeles might not do much for the neighborhood, so when something good happens that calls for a lamb slaughter, who ya gonna call? Relatives in Iran, that's who. Lambs are now slaughtered long distance and distributed to the poor in Iran. Your son bought a Lexus? There goes a lamb. The grandson graduated from UCLA law school? Don't forget the lamb.

For my wedding, the Iranian caterer told us that for an extra $250, which in Iran buys an entire flock of sheep plus the sheepherder's wages, he would roast a lamb and present it as a centerpiece. My response was, "Oh God, no." But it's not like the bride's opinion stands a chance against tradition.

With more fanfare than my own entrance got, the result was wheeled out at the beginning of dinner. François and I gasped. There on the cart was, not a lamb, but a lamb carcass, all the meat having been already carved off. On top of its skull was a conical party hat, and where its eyes had once been sat a pair of sunglasses. This creature did not belong at a wedding but on the cover of a Stephen King novel. Father Christopher announced that he was ready to perform the last rites, a perfectly funny Catholic joke wasted on this crowd.

Dinner was followed by more dancing. The D.J. played everything from Persian songs to Top Forty hits to salsa. The dance floor remained full until the time came to throw the bouquet. This is not an Iranian tradition, but any ritual that might lead to finding a husband is quickly and readily adopted into my culture. With all eligible females holding their breath, I threw my bouquet, then turned around to see who the next bride would be. There, standing at *my* reception, at *my* wedding, was a complete stranger holding *my* bouquet of yellow orchids. As the photographer scrambled to take her picture, I found my mother to ask her who that was. "That's Soheila, the daughter of Mojdeh *khanom*, who is baby-sitting your aunt Zari's grandkids tonight. She wants to get married, but she's really tall so it's hard to find an Iranian husband so your aunt Zari brought her thinking that she might meet someone at your wedding, although personally I don't think so. She really is too tall."

I could only hope that my wedding would work a bit of magic for this uninvited guest. I like to think that she eventually found a husband, a tall Iranian doctor maybe, or perhaps a short Mexican businessman with a big heart, or a medium-built Irish Catholic book vendor whose family thinks she's the best thing that ever happened to their son. But regardless of her husband's ethnicity, one thing's for sure. If she did get married, there are a couple fewer lambs in Iran.

I Feel the Earth Move

Under My Feet

After getting married, François and I moved to San Francisco, where we rented an apartment on the top floor of a four-story building. The building was a quiet one, and the tenants mainly kept to themselves. The second floor was populated entirely by old women living alone. Every morning, each of them would leave the building for a daily stroll, taking tenuous steps with the help of a walker or a caretaker.

A month after moving into our apartment, I returned home from work early one day to take care of a few errands. I was about to get into the shower when the phone rang. I put on my bathrobe and answered the phone. It was someone from UPS returning my call regarding a wedding gift that had arrived broken. As I was trying to explain that no, I did not have a receipt for the gift, the room started to shake and rattle. The pictures, which François had just hung on the wall, crashed to the floor, sending broken glass everywhere. The kitchen cabinets burst open and glasses and dishes flew out, shattering on the tile floor. As disturbing as it is to hear the sound of just one glass shattering, I was now hearing dozens of glass objects breaking in every room, at the same time. Having grown up in California, I had always heard about the Big One, the inevitable huge earthquake that awaited all of us who chose to live in sunshine instead of reason. I assumed this was it.

My first thought was that the building was going to fall. I considered putting on some clothes other than the terry cloth bathrobe I was wearing, but then I thought, "Who cares?" The floor was covered with broken glass, so I grabbed the first pair of shoes I saw, François's bunny slippers. I also took a pillow to protect my head from falling debris. As I was about to leave the apartment, I thought of my parents. I had to call them. I picked up the phone, but the line was dead. This disturbed me more than the earthquake itself.

My parents are highly evolved worriers. My mother once called me in the middle of the day to tell me to make sure I wear shoes when cleaning the attic because she had just heard about a woman who, while cleaning her attic barefoot, was bitten by a rare brown spider whose venom cut off the circulation to her extremities. Consequently, the woman's nose fell off. It was pointless for me to remind my mother that I do not have an attic.

My parents do not limit themselves to worrying about things that have actually happened. Dreams are also fair game. I often get phone calls with detailed descriptions of a dream, followed by "So naturally, I had to call to make sure you were okay and there wasn't a reason why I dreamed of you trapped in a canoe with a blue turtle." If worrying were an Olympic sport, my parents' faces would have graced the Wheaties box a long time ago.

I tried the phone again, but it was still dead. I left my apartment and started walking down the stairs, holding the pillow on my head with both hands. The quake had activated the fire alarm, so the hallways were ringing. As I reached the second floor, I saw one of the old ladies standing in her doorway, shaking uncontrollably. Her face had no color. My first thought was that this person was about to have a heart attack. "Let's leave the building. There are probably going to be aftershocks," I told her. She just stared at me. I put my arms around her tiny shaking body and started stroking her head. She was trembling like a little bird. In a thick Eastern European accent, she haltingly told me that she just wanted to go back to her apartment.

Still holding and stroking her, I stepped into her apartment and sat down on the sofa. I told her that everything was okay and that we had nothing to worry about. I did not believe a word I was saying, but she apparently did. After a while, the color started slowly coming back into her face. I again suggested leaving the building, but she refused. By the time I decided to leave, she looked normal and was telling me how glad she was that her favorite lamp had not broken. Before stepping out of her apartment, I asked her if I could try using her phone.

I picked up the phone and heard a dial tone. I called my parents and was greeted cheerfully by my father, who clearly had not heard about the earthquake.

"Baba," I said, "there was a big earthquake, but I just wanted to let you know that I'm okay."

"No problem," he answered cheerfully. "How's everything else?"

My father was not grasping the gravity of the situation and I had no idea how to describe the earthquake without the handy Richter scale number. "It was a *big* earthquake. Everything broke," I told him.

"Don't worry," he said. "Things are replaceable."

"Just know I'm okay," I said. "I gotta go."

As soon as I hung up, I thought that I should also call my in-laws, who at the time were living in Marin County, forty-five minutes from San Francisco.

Ever since marrying François, I had clung to the notion that my mother-in-law, in a moment of enlightenment, would cast aside her prejudices and join François and me in celebrating our union. I imagined us preparing elaborate Christmas dinners together and her telling me for the hundredth time how narrow-minded she had been before getting to know me. And for the hundredth time, I would tell her that I forgave her.

I dialed my in-laws' number. My mother-in-law picked up the phone. I was pretty sure this would be the moment of bonding. It would go something like this: "Oh, dear, Firoozeh, this earthquake shook me up and made me realize what a fool I've been! How could I have judged you because of your nationality? What was I thinking? Muslims, Jews, Catholics, we're all the same. Imagine, it took me this long to wake up and see that we all laugh the same laughs and cry the same tears. Please forgive me!"

I got it almost right:

My mother-in-law asked whether her china had broken.

Before the wedding, François had discovered in his parents' garage two large boxes of Limoges china that had never been unpacked. François had never seen these dishes. He assumed they were yet another box of inherited dishes that his parents owned but had never gotten around to using. He asked his mother whether he could have them. In a rare moment of generosity, she said yes.

For weeks following the Loma Prieta earthquake, building inspectors measured the damage and labeled structures with green, yellow, or red stickers. Ours was given a yellow sticker, which unlike a red sticker, meant that we could return to our homes.

However, many repairs needed to be made. The elevator had to be fixed for the elderly residents, but otherwise we didn't expect much; we had come to accept that our landlord's idea of maintenance was cashing the rent checks.

One evening a few weeks after the earthquake, there was a knock on our door. I opened the door and standing there was the elderly lady I had met during the earthquake. She was holding a chocolate Bundt cake. As soon as she saw me, she burst into tears. Handing me the cake, she took out a wad of tissue and said, "I just vanted to tell you," but she got no further. Her sobs got louder. "I just vanted to tell you," she said again, "dat you saved my *life*. My name eez Golda Rubenshtein and you saved my *life*."

She continued to sob. I thanked her and told her that she had actually saved my parents' life, since her phone was the only one working and . . . She didn't let me finish. "I just vanted to tank you and make sure you knew that you saved my *life*."

I thanked her for the cake again and told her I was glad that she was fine. I also thanked her again for letting me use her phone.

For a week after the earthquake, all the phones in our building had been dead. My parents later told me that after my phone call, they had turned on the news and seen the devastation. "Had it not been for your phone call," they always say, "we would've worried ourselves to death." Golda's was the only phone in the entire building that had been working.

A month later, Golda made another surprise visit, this time bringing only half a chocolate Bundt cake. Once again, I opened my door and she burst into tears. Handing me the cake, she took out a wad of tissue. In between sobs, she said, "I called my son and I says, 'Yakov,' I says, 'Yakov, an *angel* came to me. An *angel* saved my *life*.'" Listening to her own reenactment of the phone call, she sobbed louder.

I thanked her for the cake and told her how grateful I was for what she had done for my parents, but she didn't want to hear any of it.

Every month, like clockwork, Golda came to our door with half a chocolate Bundt cake, a heart full of gratitude, and eyes full of tears. One time when I wasn't home, she had encountered François and asked him whether he knew that he was married to an *angel*. She had also told him that he was too skinny and she was going to fatten him up.

Fortunately or unfortunately, I wasn't sure which, my mother-in-law's china had not broken. The earthquake did, however, make her rethink her impulsive burst of generosity. This did not surprise us. I would not be singing "Kumbaya" with this woman any time soon.

As beautiful as they were, two words now described these dishes: *bad karma*. François wanted to give them back and forget the whole thing. I was willing to get rid of them, but I did not want to give them back to his mother. I also didn't want to sell them; I figured their bad karma would extend to any money that we made from them.

A home for families of children undergoing long-term treatment at a nearby hospital was having a benefit auction. I contacted the organization: Were they interested in a seventy-piece set of antique Limoges? They were.

After the auction, we received a letter thanking us for our donation and informing us of the selling price. We were thrilled that somebody now owned a beautiful set of china that came with no strings attached. More important, we were happy to have helped out a family that was dealing with a gravely ill child. And, if feeling good wasn't enough of a reward, we were now considered "major donors" to the organization.

For the next few years, we were honored guests at a handful of dinners for major donors, all of which were held at elaborate homes where the paintings on the walls were not reproductions. These were catered events with valet parking. At the time, we owned one car, a Honda with a large ding on the side. I always suggested to François that perhaps we should park our car a few blocks away and walk. François refused, insisting that, should he suddenly wake up and find himself a multimillionaire, he would like to think of himself as the type who wouldn't be a slave to status symbols, the type who would still remember the little people and the cars driven by the little people. "Plus," he added, "maybe the valets will get mixed up and give us a BMW."

At these dinners, we met all sorts of people whose names graced museums and large institutions. These were people who had not had a financial worry in three generations. At age twenty-six, François and I were by far the youngest guests. Knowing that our days at these swanky shindigs were numbered, we tried to make the most of them by trying each and every one of the desserts.

We never did tell my mother-in-law about the china. She never accepted our marriage; even the birth of our children did not soften her. We eventually stopped having contact with her.

The Limoges set has brought us more joy in its absence than it ever did in our cupboards. Of course, we no longer own a set of china to pass down to our kids, but that's okay. François and I plan on giving our children something more valuable, the simple truth that the best way to go through life is to be a major donor of kindness. We'll tell them that it's possible to own a whole bunch of beautiful, valuable things and still be miserable. But sometimes just having a recipe for chocolate Bundt cake can make a person far, far happier.

A Nose by Any Other Name

When I was a student at Berkeley, I found myself fascinated by a certain librarian there. This woman had the ugliest nose I had ever seen. It was as if God, in a moment of confusion, had switched her nose with the beak of an exotic bird. I suspected that somewhere deep in the rain forests of Brazil, high in a mango tree, lived a toucan with a human nose.

What triggered my fascination wasn't the sheer majesty of the librarian's nose, but her abundant confidence. This woman carried herself like a beauty queen. As I watched her go about her duties in her self-assured manner, I couldn't help but wonder, "Why doesn't she have a complex?"

In Iranian culture, a woman's nose is much more than a breathing device; it is her destiny. A girl with an ugly nose learns early on to dream of one thing only—a skilled plastic surgeon. Only the poorest families do not intervene to correct nature's nasal missteps. No amount of charm, talent, or intelligence can make a girl overcome an ugly nose; it simply must be fixed.

I am descended from two types of noses. On my father's side, the noses are big but otherwise perfectly reasonable. God just

didn't know when to stop a good thing. The noses in my maternal lineage are all large and hooked. Gonzo, on *Sesame Street*,
bears an uncanny resemblance to my mother's side of the family.
I grew up thinking that it was normal to yell "Not the profile!"
whenever a picture was being taken. Mine is the kind of nose
that enabled me to impress fellow high school students with my
ability to balance a pencil and eraser between my nose and
mouth. This enviable contortion act pretty much sealed my fate
as the type of girl who never had to worry about buying a prom
dress.

When I was small, all eyes were on my nose. I was considered
a cute little girl, but whenever anyone commented on my looks,
someone, usually my mother, would say, "We'll see." Everyone
knew what that meant. History is full of girls who were cute one
day and then boom, the nose grew. And my female relatives had
known them all. They continued their nose watch, tracking my
rhinal growth like traders tracking stock on Wall Street.

By the time I was an adolescent, it was clear that I had been
somewhat spared. I had a hooked nose lite. I resembled my maternal relatives, but the nose wasn't quite bad enough to invite
comparison to a puppet. The consensus among my female relatives was that even though my nose wasn't horrific, it could use a
little improvement. "You just need the tip removed."

When I was eighteen, my father and I headed off to a consul-
tation with a plastic surgeon, "the best in Newport Beach." As I
sat in this man's well-appointed office and looked at the expan-
sive ocean view, I wondered how he could take himself seriously.
Judging by the framed diplomas all over the walls, he had spent
many years studying at prestigious medical establishments. Here
was somebody who could be saving a life somewhere, but instead
he was looking forward to lopping off the tip of my nose. As he

explained the procedure, what bothered me the most wasn't the idea of having my nose broken, but having my nose broken by *him*. I just didn't respect him enough.

My father was relieved that I had decided against a nose job. He thought it was way too expensive. "You can buy me a car instead," I suggested. "Your nose is fine," he replied, "and you don't need a car."

Despite the ominous warnings from my female relatives that noses keep growing well into adulthood, I managed to graduate from college, get married, and have children, all with my original nose. I hadn't actually thought about my nasal imperfections in years; after two pregnancies, I had found other body parts far worthier of obsession.

I had, however, thought about the Toucan. Whenever anyone complained about his nose, I always shared the story of the confident librarian who had overcome her formidable rhinal challenge. Naturally, people wanted to know why she had so much confidence. "I don't know. She just did," I always replied. Little did I dream that I would someday find out.

About twenty years after my last sighting of the Toucan, François and I and our two kids were on our way to a motel for a week. Our house was on the market, and the real estate agent felt that it would sell more quickly if we weren't in it. Somehow toys scattered throughout the house and toilets that the little ones had forgotten to flush are not considered a marketing boon. François and I cleaned the house, removed all the extra things we had stuffed in our closets, put fresh vases full of flowers everywhere, and left.

We arrived at the local motel just in time to go to bed. While we were putting the kids to sleep, François was called in to work. As soon as he left, every article I had ever read about crimes being committed in motel rooms came flooding back to me. I was convinced that the moment I fell asleep, a disgruntled ex-employee who had managed to keep the master key would come back to avenge himself. I was not going to be able to sleep until my husband returned. Desperate for a distraction, I turned on the TV. Since we don't have a television in our house, I assumed it would be fairly easy to find something entertaining, if only for the novelty. I started flipping channels, avoiding the in-depth profiles of serial murderers, zipping past the sitcoms, past the infomercials selling juicers, past Susan Lucci selling shampoo. Just as I was thinking *Thank God I don't have a television so I don't have to watch this crap,* all of a sudden there she was on the screen. The Toucan. She looked exactly the same except for a few more gray hairs. I assumed that this was a show about the Dewey decimal system or recent donations to the UC–Berkeley library. But suddenly, the camera panned back and I saw that the Toucan was *completely naked.*

My father had always told me that a college education would give me endless opportunities. I never realized that seeing the librarians naked would be one of them.

I was intrigued and repulsed at the same time. I looked to make sure my children were sleeping. They were still at the age when they readily announced every detail of our life to perfect strangers. "Mommy watches naked women on television" might not get them into the best preschools. I hoped that François would not come home and think I was hiding some big secret.

I sat back to watch the interview, more awake now than before. The naked Toucan had startled me more than any ax-wielding disgruntled ex-employee. According to the interview, the Toucan was a member of a nudist colony in Northern California. This in-depth profile covered not only her experiences as a nudist, but also the experiences of the other nudists.

The Toucan talked extensively about coming to accept herself *as she is.* She didn't refer to her nose, but that's what I was thinking about. She said that she had struggled with low self-esteem her whole life until she discovered nudism. Somehow she had shed her clothes and her poor self-image simultaneously, a concept that could truly put a dent in the world of cosmetic surgery. How odd, I thought, that I had so wondered about this woman's self-confidence and my question was being answered on an obscure cable show in a cheap motel at midnight.

The Toucan continued listing the virtues of nudity, how being naked took away all pretenses and left others to see her for *who she really was.* I had always thought that conversation revealed who people really were. But apparently seeing their saggy body parts could actually tell me a whole lot more.

The other members of the colony said basically the same thing as the Toucan, although she was by far the most articulate, not to mention the best-looking. Before this show, I had assumed that watching a group of naked people would be erotic in some way. Not this group. I was not the only one who had not gone to the prom.

The show ended with a scene of all the nudists sitting around a campfire laughing and bonding. Watching this jovial group, I found myself overcome with sadness. I couldn't help but think of all the Iranian women who had paid to have their noses broken and reshaped just so someone might find them worthy of love. I thought of all the little girls I had known who had learned to cringe at their own reflections. I remembered how much I admired Jane Fonda's nose when I was in fourth grade in Tehran, and how much I hated my own. Thinking of all that wasted energy, I wanted to scream and tell my fellow countrymen and countrywomen that a nose by any other name is just a nose. It does not hold the soul, for no matter how big our noses may be, our souls are far, far bigger.

My husband was quite surprised to find me awake at two in the morning when he returned from work.

"What have you been doing?" he asked.

"Watching television."

"But you hate television," he reminded me.

"Believe me," I said, "there are some interesting shows nowadays."

Judges Paid Off

My brother Farshid travels frequently on business. Having accumulated enough mileage to travel to the moon and back, business class, he regularly treats family and friends to free trips to faraway lands. After our first year of marriage, he offered François and me tickets to the Bahamas, if we were interested. We were interested.

The timing was perfect. Both François and I had just changed jobs and we each had a two-week break. Neither of us had ever been to the Bahamas, but how can you go wrong with white sandy beaches, warm water, and swaying palm trees?

We landed in Nassau, where we had reservations for two nights. We had not made any further plans, choosing instead a more adventurous approach. "Let's get there and see which island beckons us" was our motto.

There's a fine line between a sense of adventure and stupidity, and we had crossed that line. Once in Nassau, we discovered that there was no island beckoning us. We had arrived smack dab in the middle of spring break, and the Bahamas were full, full of people far more intelligent than we who had already made reservations on every boat or plane leaving Nassau for the other islands. We were stuck.

Perhaps it is unfair to judge any place during spring break. After all, the students who flock to these resorts are generally not the brightest lights in the American galaxy. These are people for whom a vacation does not officially begin until they have thrown up a couple of times. It seems like such a waste for them to fly to the Bahamas, or anywhere else, since they can just as easily go to a motel in their own neck of the woods and simply pass out for a week. It would serve this country better if these types could have their passports stamped "Domestic Travel Only," thereby limiting the damage they do as national embarrassments.

During our first night, we were kept up till dawn thanks to the drunken festivities taking place in all the rooms around us and in the hallway. We complained to the management: for $180 a night, we should be entitled to get some sleep. Sorry, they said. Hang loose.

We spent the next day desperately trying to find a way to leave Nassau and the spring breakers, a locale that would have inspired Dante to add a tenth ring to his hell. Every bus, plane, and boat was full. We walked around town, asking the locals if they had any idea how we could get to any of the islands. The locals all shook their heads, then asked us if we wanted to buy coke. They weren't talking about the fizzy drink.

By the end of the first day, I was ready to cry. I had seen no swaying palm trees, just swaying drunks. There was no sea life, just piles of beer-bloated students passed out on the beach. They did resemble groups of elephant seals from far away, but the travel brochure had shown dolphins.

We returned to the hotel and asked the security guard

whether he had any advice. He suggested we go to the post office and inquire about the mail boats that ferried goods from Nassau to the other islands; they were willing to take passengers, space permitting. We also asked him why the police didn't do anything about all the people trying to sell coke on every corner. "The police are often in on it," he told us. "We have a lot of wealthy cops in the Bahamas."

The guidebook that we had purchased in the States listed all the official mail boats. With guidebook in hand, we arrived at the post office and were told there was only one boat, the *Spanish Rose*, leaving during the next two weeks, and it was departing the next morning at seven. I immediately looked it up in my guidebook. It wasn't listed.

"It's not on the official list," I informed François. "It's probably a drug boat. I'm not going."

"What do you think is going to happen?" François asked.

"We'll be next week's headlines. 'Dismembered Bodies Discovered. Camera Equipment Missing.' I am not going," I repeated.

We stood arguing on the street corner for a while; then François approached a policeman and asked him whether he had ever heard of a mail boat called the *Spanish Rose*. "Of course," the policeman said enthusiastically.

"See," François said. "Are you convinced it's legitimate?"

I was shocked at the naïveté of this Frenchman. "The cop is in on it," I whispered. "He probably lives in a big house on a hill with an ocean view."

"That's it," François said. "I am going to come here tomorrow morning at six. You do what you want. I, however, will be boarding the boat."

"Fine," I said.

The next morning we showed up early and found a group of Bahamian families ready to board the *Spanish Rose*. It looked perfectly safe. François asked whether I was embarrassed by the previous day's display of paranoia. "I don't recall," I said, doing my best imitation of a politician on trial. We boarded and found a spot among the crates of tomatoes, potatoes, and eggs and several cages of live chickens.

The boat ride was straight out of a Jacques Cousteau special. We passed by small islands with white beaches and swaying palm trees. The water, which was teeming with fish, changed colors from turquoise to jade to cobalt. Overhead, the cloudless sky presented us with yet another magnificent shade of blue. This was the Bahamas we had dreamed about.

Four hours later, we arrived at the island of Spanish Wells. Our guidebook mentioned only that this small island, inhabited by lobster fishermen, was named after the Spanish sailors who used to come ashore for fresh water.

"Excuse us," we asked the first person we saw at the dock. "Can you tell us where to find a taxi?"

The old man looked us over. "Where are you going?"

"We'd like to find a hotel," we answered cheerfully.

"I'll give you a ride," he said.

We put the suitcase in the trunk and buckled ourselves in. Thirty seconds later, he announced, "Here we are."

He refused to accept money but he did tell us to come to his restaurant, where he served "the best fried turtle on the islands." François's eyes lit up. "Gross," I thought. I draw the line at any animal that features prominently in Aesop's fables.

The receptionist asked us how long we were planning on staying. "About ten nights," we said.

She opened the large reservation book, running her forefinger down each page. She never said a word. She didn't look at us, just turned the pages s-l-o-w-l-y. "That's it," I thought. "They're booked full and we're stranded."

Finally she spoke. "This way," she said.

The receptionist, who was also the bellhop, carried our bag to our room, then waited for a tip. We asked her whether the hotel was full. "All the rooms are vacant," she said. They remained that way during our entire stay.

Our room was right on the white, sandy beach. The calm blue ocean filled the horizon. Except for a few palm trees, there was nothing else on the beach.

We put down our bags and decided to go look for a place to eat. Walking up and down the island, we noticed that the streets were empty—no tourists, no locals. The atmosphere reminded me of a book I had read in junior high about a boy who was the only survivor of an atomic bomb and had to rely on his wits to survive. I couldn't remember anything else about the book, but I knew that if I had to rely on my wits to survive, I was far worse off than the turtles. We went back to our hotel, but the receptionist wasn't there. That was because she was now the waitress at the hotel's restaurant.

We were seated after a few minutes and given menus with pictures of lobsters on them. "That's what I want!" said François. "Sorry," said the receptionist-bellhop-waitress, "but it's not lobster season."

We ordered conch chowder and sandwiches. The service was quite good, but then again we were the only customers in the restaurant. The food, though, was unbelievably expensive. We later found out that this was because everything has to be brought to Spanish Wells by boat. A box of Cheerios at the island's grocery store, Pinder Market, cost $6.50.

While we were eating lunch, the owner of the hotel, a British man, came to say hello. He was thrilled to see us, especially when he found out we were staying for ten days. He proceeded to tell us a few facts about the island—how, unlike other Bahamians, the inhabitants of Spanish Wells are all white, and how they work six months out of the year catching lobster, earning at least $100,000 per year. This did explain the number of satellite dishes we had seen on our walk.

I asked the owner what he did before he moved to Spanish Wells. "Well," he said, "I worked somewhere you have never heard of."

That's what I say whenever anybody asks me where I was born.

"Where is that?" I asked him.

"Abadan, Iran," he said.

I had to hold myself back from an a cappella rendition of "It's a Small World." It turns out not only did this man live in Abadan, he worked at the same company as my father, the National Iranian Oil Company. He knew my old neighborhood, the local clubhouse, and Alfi's, the general store where I bought all my tea sets.

After lunch, we set out for a walk along the shore. Big, heavy conch shells littered the beach. "I know what I'm bringing back from this trip!" I told François. "Just so you know," he said. "You collect it, you carry it home."

We saw no other tourists on the island. François spent his days reading murder mysteries while I schemed of ways to bring back my growing conch shell collection. Taking breaks from doing nothing, we went on long walks, discovering such unusual sights as a drug plane that had crashed years ago on its way from Colombia. Unfamiliar with the nuances of the cocaine trade, we had no idea that it was a drug plane when we first saw it. That evening, we were enlightened about its unique history by our receptionist-bellhop-waitress-historian. Later, we returned to take pictures in front of its hollowed interior where the bags of cocaine had been stored. This was a classic example of travel brochures leaving out the best tidbits.

During our walks, we also discovered the Pinder Restaurant, the Pinder Bakery, and the Pinder Gas Station. Back at the hotel, we asked the owner why most of the businesses were called Pinder. He took out the island's phone book. Almost everyone in the book, all twenty pages, was named Pinder. Apparently the island had been settled by two families, the Pinder family and the Pinder family. "And they had kids and made more Pinders," he added.

Halfway through our stay, as we were eating yet another frighteningly expensive meal, the owner of the hotel approached our table, sat down, and asked us if we were enjoying our stay. His sudden interest in us made me think that he was about to ask us for something. It reminded me of when I was six years old and Farshid would tell me what a wonderful sister I was and then ask me to share my Kit Kat bar with him. Sure enough, the Englishman asked us whether we would be willing to do a favor for the people of Spanish Wells. *Good God*, I thought. *Drug smuggling.*

He continued, "Every year, the girls of Spanish Wells compete in a beauty pageant. It's the biggest event of the year and every girl dreams of winning the title and qualifying for the Miss Bahamas pageant. The problem is that we can never find judges who are not related to the contestants, since as you've noticed, it's a small island. We were wondering if you two would do us the honor of serving as judges in this year's pageant."

I hate beauty pageants. This may have to do with the fact that

I was one of those girls who learn early on that they will have to rely on their brains to open doors. It took me years to overcome the beauty expectations of Iranian culture and a few more years to overcome growing up in Newport Beach, where the standard of beauty involves rigorous exercise, bottles of hydrogen peroxide, and silicone. There was no way I was going to dip my toe in the dysfunctional pond of beauty pageants.

As if reading my mind, the Englishman continued, "It's not just about beauty—there's a talent competition and a question-and-answer segment. Please consider this, since otherwise, we don't have enough judges."

There wasn't much we could say. "We'll do it," we said.

"Splendid," he exclaimed.

The next morning, when the receptionist-bellhop-waitress-historian-maid came to clean the room, she greeted us with unusual enthusiasm.

"So I heard you will be judging the pageant this year! I competed three times."

"I thought you can only compete once in a beauty pageant," I said.

"We don't have a lot of girls on the island, so you can keep trying."

The following afternoon, hundreds of residents of Spanish Wells stood on the beach to watch the arrival of a small motorboat. I had not seen this many people since we landed. As the boat approached, I could see a woman wearing a purple hat with large purple feathers waving at everyone. The crowd went wild.

As she gingerly stepped off the boat, we were told this was a former Miss Bahamas who had come to be a pageant judge. The fourth judge would be the son of a wealthy Canadian family that owned a large house on the island.

The next night, François and I, the former Miss Bahamas, and the rich Canadian, who happened to be drunk, met with the pageant's organizer. She breathlessly explained that there would be a bathing suit competition, a talent competition during which each girl would have to represent some aspect of life in the Bahamas, and a question-and-answer segment. This woman was so excited, it became obvious that the pageant was far more than just an entertainment. We were being asked to determine the course of the future for these young girls. I had always known that I would make a great god, but now that I had the opportunity, I wanted to run away.

We were escorted to the pageant by the Englishman, who, like a fisherman bragging about his large catch, let everyone know he had reeled in two judges for the competition. The auditorium was packed with screaming people holding signs declaring their choice for the evening's winner. "Miss Spanish Wells = Chantal!"

Seated between the former Miss Bahamas and the rich, drunk Canadian, surrounded by screaming islanders, I could only hope that Pinder Market sold antacid. I had the same dreadful feeling I'd had the last time I was strapped into a roller coaster, although at least that experience lasted only a few minutes. If this evening ever ended, I would be adding "judging beauty pageants" to my list of things never to try again, right under "gymnastics classes" and "blood sausage."

The emcee got onstage and managed to quiet the crowd. He announced the names of the six girls competing for the title. Four of them were Pinders. After each name, he had to pause a few minutes to let the cheering die down. At least if I ever compete in a pageant, my large, fertile Middle Eastern family will guarantee me a win for largest cheering section.

The girls then all filed onto the stage, which led to more cheering and screaming and sign waving. They drew straws to determine the order in which they would compete.

First there was the talent competition, during which they were supposed to represent the Bahamas in some meaningful way. Contestant No. 1 came out wearing a lobster costume that can be kindly described as homemade. "I represent the lobster industry," she began. As she spewed out lobster statistics, her stuffed lobster arms and legs bounced up and down, giving the impression that she was waving to eight people simultaneously.

Contestant No. 2 came out covered with a fisherman's net adorned with seashells and fake kelp. She represented the ocean and all that it had to give.

Contestant No. 3 wore a diver's suit, complete with fins, and presented an ode to the coral.

Contestant No. 4 wore a flag of the Bahamas and sang a song that I assume was the national anthem. I had no idea what the song was supposed to sound like, although I was quite sure it wasn't supposed to sound like what I was hearing.

Contestant No. 5, dressed as the sun, wore a yellow leotard complete with a swim cap on which Styrofoam rays of sunshine had been glued. She discussed the beautiful weather in the Bahamas, sharing statistics on the number of days of sunshine and inches of rain.

The last contestant wore a blue dress and read a poem she had written about the ocean. "You are blue, we love you, what would we do, without you . . ."

By the end of that segment, I wished Scotty could beam me up. Instead, the swimsuit competition began.

Swimsuit competitions go against everything that is right and decent in this world. We're told that beauty is on the inside and that who we are matters far more than what we look like. But could you please just put on this bikini and walk around on high heels so I can judge your inner beauty? I don't know which was worse, to be a contestant or a judge. I wanted to stand up on the table and tell the girls to take off their high heels and hurl them at the organizers of this event, demanding that the pageant be replaced by a spelling bee. Instead, I just sat there and prayed for the end.

For the last part, the deep-question segment, the girls had to answer a question drawn out of a hat.

"What would you do if you were selected as Miss Bahamas?"

"If you could solve one problem, what would it be?"

I'd been hoping the questions would be more interesting.

"If you were to design a theme park around the crashed drug plane, what would you call it?"

"Besides turtles, can you think of any other endangered species that we could cut up and fry?"

Finally, the judges were herded into a small room to discuss the contestants. The former Miss Bahamas, a stunning and intelligent woman, and the only person in the world who could wear a hat with large purple feathers and still look good, reminded us that we needed to pick someone who was articulate, since she felt that this was a major part of the pageant. François and I agreed with her. The Canadian had nothing to say; he apparently could not recall the previous two hours. The rest of us decided that the talent competition had not yielded a clear winner. The Canadian nodded. We decided to ignore the swimsuit competition, calling it irrelevant. The Canadian nodded. We then agreed that there was only one articulate contestant and she should be the winner. The Canadian did not nod again, because he had nodded off. We woke him up and went back into the auditorium, where once again we were greeted with cheers and screams and sign waving. Right then and there I gave up all desire of ever becoming a rock star. It was just too loud.

The girl we had selected was undoubtedly the underdog. She was quite overweight, she was the least physically attractive, and she had the smallest cheering section. She was, however, the most articulate. This may have been because she was considerably older than the other contestants and probably a repeater. The crowd's favorite was a girl named Chantal, who was by far the prettiest and the best-looking in a bathing suit, but we were looking for depth, not beauty.

As soon as the emcee appeared, the crowd fell silent. People started huddling close together, anticipating the next opportunity to scream. The emcee said a few words about how all the girls are so qualified and how hard it must have been to select just one. To a completely hushed audience, he then announced the runners-up, whom we had pretty much picked at random. There were three girls left; everyone assumed the winner was Chantal. He then announced the winner.

I can barely recall the next few moments, because I was having a panic attack. The instant the winner's name was announced, everyone screamed, but this was not a joyous scream. This was a bad scream, the kind of scream that is usually emitted by mobs waving clubs and leads to eventual inclusion in history books. The audience was chanting "No way! No way!" Chantal stood onstage crying. The winner and her mother, who looked just like her daughter but more overweight, came and thanked us. "We can't believe it!" they said. Neither, apparently, could anybody else.

François and I managed to get out of the auditorium, running all the way back to our hotel. "They're going to kill us," I said to

François. "That's what you said about the mail boat," François said.

We went into our room and started getting ready for bed, although I was quite sure I would not be sleeping much that night.

"What's that noise?" I asked François.

"What noise?"

"Listen," I said.

We could hear a distinct rumbling that was getting louder and louder. François opened the door, then immediately shut it. "It's nothing," he said.

François has many talents, but lying is not one of them.

By the time I got to the door, I could hear the distinct chanting of a large, angry crowd. "Judges paid off! Judges paid off!"

The protest went on well into the night. I could not fall asleep, knowing that if the mobs stormed our dinky hotel room, my only weapon was a collection of conch shells. I tried to imagine how my parents would be contacted to claim our bodies. "It was a violent incident involving a beauty pageant," they would be told. It was a long night, during which my husband slept like a log.

If I Were a Rich Man

In Abadan, we never had to think about money, not because we were rich, but because the National Iranian Oil Company took care of all our needs. Employees received free furnished housing; the size and amenities were based on years of experience and education. Plumbing problems, electrical problems, and leaky roofs were fixed free of charge. Schools, doctors, and even buses cost nothing. For entertainment, everyone converged at the local clubhouse for bingo, swimming, movies, and concerts. Except for food, it was all free of charge. The club also held Persian New Year celebrations, Christmas parties, and even an annual *bal masqué* with an award given for best costume. My parents and Aunt Sedigeh and Uncle Abdullah always dressed up as villagers, and every year they didn't win. In 1957, an employee of the fire department won with his rendition of a spaceship passenger.

As an engineer with a graduate degree, my father was entitled to a three-bedroom house with a huge backyard complete with a vegetable garden and chickens. Each day, I made my rounds, verifying whether the carrots, corn, radishes, or green beans were ready to eat. Afterward, I checked for insects, keeping track of all the creatures that shared our garden. My mother found my interest in bugs an odd and somewhat disturbing hobby for a little girl. My daughter shares that fascination with things that creep and crawl, and I tell her that a career in entomology awaits her.

Our front yard in Abadan was filled with roses, jasmine, and narcissus. Next to the flower beds stood a large covered swing. Every evening, when the stifling heat lifted, we would sit outside on the swing, sipping cherry drinks or Pepsi and eating salted sunflower seeds. Our evenings were often punctuated with the sound of our neighbor's shrill voice: "Jeemee! Jeemee!" Her husband's name was not Jimmy, but Javad, but our neighbor had seen a few too many American movies and had decided to anglicize her husband's name, adding a bit of exoticism to our neck of the woods. Not to be outdone, we acquired a stray dog and named it Jimmy. And this is how, on any given evening, one could hear not one but two families calling for their respective Jeemees.

When we first came to America, not only did we have to adjust to paying for everything ("The plumber charges for just *looking* at the problem?"), we had to pay with American currency. In 1972, one dollar was worth seven toumans, or seventy rials. This meant that a package of Oscar Mayer bologna cost not two dollars but fourteen toumans. Tomatoes were not fifty cents per pound, but three and a half toumans. Nothing could be purchased without an automatic conversion to Iranian currency, followed by the requisite "Ooh, that's a lot."

Little did we know that what seemed expensive when we first came to America would appear to be a downright bargain after the Iranian Revolution. Political upheaval is rarely good for the economy; in 1979, the value of Iranian currency took a nosedive. One dollar eventually was worth eight hundred toumans or eight thousand rials. The two-dollar package of Oscar Mayer bologna now cost sixteen hundred toumans, the price of a small Persian rug before the revolution. Even Iranians who used to spend money freely now had to think twice before all purchases.

My father has always been a thrifty man, but our financial problems after the revolution thrust him onto a new plane of existence, a universe with the motto "I'll fix it myself." A white lab coat and stethoscope do not a doctor make, and a dozen trips to the Sears hardware department do not a handyman make. But, short of drilling for oil or hunting squirrel, my father came to believe that he could take care of all his family's needs. His engineering background, combined with his *Time-Life Home Repair and Improvement* (a fourteen-volume set), convinced him that he could address any leak, drip, rattle, or clog. Any objection or doubt we expressed led him to recount the story of how he had built a radio when he was a teenager. When challenged with the point that installing tile is perhaps different from building a radio, he would always reply, "Not really."

Strolling through our house, one sees ample evidence of my father's can-do spirit. So what if the hot water comes out of the faucet marked "Cold"? That's nothing compared to what a plumber would have charged to fix the sink! And the duct tape covering the holes in the kitchen wall? Who is going to notice those? As for the way the wallpaper in the bathroom doesn't match, let's not get too picky. It's just a bathroom, not a dining room. Should Time-Life publish a *Do-It-Yourself Guide to Medical Procedures,* my mother and I will be leaving the country.

If my father limited his handyman skills to his own humble abode, that would be fine. Unfortunately, Kazem Appleseed insists on sharing his gifts with the rest of us. Having "fixed" everything in his own house, he has moved on to his children's.

My brother Farshid is an executive in a high-tech firm. Unlike our father, Farshid has no problem spending money. He pays someone to wash his car, someone to hem his pants, and someone to clean his house. Not only does he have all his clothes dry cleaned, he pays extra to have his laundry picked up and dropped off at his doorstep.

During my parents' last visit to Farshid, our father initiated and completed a small project. After Farshid left for work, Kazem strolled to the hardware store and picked up a few items. He then spent the entire day spackling and painting.

After twelve hours at work, my brother returned home to discover a blotchy pattern on all the walls of his twenty-fourth-floor penthouse. "What *is* this?"

"Try to find a crack or hole," my father challenged him. "I covered them all. There were a lot."

"*Who* asked you to do this?" my brother asked incredulously. "Where did you get this paint? It's an entirely different color from my walls."

"It's fine if you don't thank me, but for your information white paint is white paint," my father replied.

Seizing an opportunity to avenge a few of her own home repair memories, my mother chimed in, "I told him not to do it. He didn't listen. He never listens."

"Well," my father exclaimed indignantly, preparing us for the aphorism he uses like a maraschino cherry to top off all his unappreciated repair projects, "a man standing next to a river cannot appreciate water."

Luckily for my father, we weren't standing next to a river. Someone might have ended up in it.

When my husband and I bought a condominium, we invited my parents for a visit. Our home was spanking new, which meant there was nothing to repair. After a few hours, however, my father announced, "You need a medicine cabinet in the bathroom."

"We don't need a medicine cabinet in the bathroom," we replied.

"I think you do," said my father, sounding undeterred.

"We don't need one. We don't want one."

My father, like a cat, should not be left alone indoors for eight hours. Marking his territory, he purchased and installed a medicine cabinet in our bathroom while my husband and I were at work. Perhaps if it hadn't been hung crooked, François would not have been so upset.

During his next visit, my father secretly decided that our bathroom needed towel hooks. Using nails that were too long, my father pierced the door, creating towel hooks on one side, medieval blinding devices on the other.

My husband has since taken the situation into his own hands, hiding all our screwdrivers and hammers before my parents visit.

My father has never apologized for any of his handyman missteps, insisting instead that our lack of appreciation stems from deeper issues. "If I had charged you a thousand dollars for spackling and painting, you'd think it looked better," he told Farshid. He regularly tells my mother that her complaints about holes left in walls and mismatched tiles only reveal her desire to impress others, a quality that she needs to change. When my husband complained that the medicine cabinet we never wanted in the first place was crooked, my father replied, "It still holds things." His ability not to apologize for glaring mistakes would have served him well in another venue, perhaps politics; it has taught us never to complain about any problem in the house, lest my father decide to fix it. No matter how inconvenient a household malfunction might be, Kazem can always make it worse, for free.

Just as my father cannot envision actually calling a plumber for a clogged sink, he cannot understand why people eat in restaurants. For him, eating out means going to one of his sisters' houses, where not only is the food fresh, delicious, and served by people who love him and laugh at his jokes, but there is no bill at the end.

Going to a real restaurant with my father always means the same thing:

"The chicken is twelve dollars? Does that mean we get the whole chicken? Let's see. They have two, four, six, eight, ten . . . twenty tables here, four people per table average, each ordering the chicken dish, let's say three seatings per evening, multiply that by eight hundred toumans . . . Geez, I should've opened a restaurant."

These calculations never include the costs of running a restaurant, just the supposed profits. Needless to say, we never dare order drinks with my father, since a $2.50 glass of lemonade, which requires at maximum three lemons at ten cents each, plus a little sugar, multiplied by eight hundred toumans . . . We always drink water, tap of course, since bottled water would most certainly lead to a whole other lecture beginning with how he grew up drinking the water in Ahwaz and is none the worse for it and you can multiply that by eight hundred.

Like a caterpillar morphing into a butterfly, my father magically transforms into Daddy Warbucks as soon as he sets foot in Iran. This is because, in Iran, my father is a millionaire. During their annual visits, he and my mother stay at the former Sheraton in Tehran, a hotel they could have never afforded without a complete devaluation of Iranian currency. Each year, my relatives in Iran, a country whose people are known for hospitality, beg my parents to stay with them, but my father refuses, explaining that staying in a suite is not something he can afford anywhere else. The relatives come and visit him, and he treats them all to lavish restaurant meals, leaving huge tips for all the employees.

Once my father accepted that his monthly pension from thirty-three years of employment with the National Iranian Oil Company would buy him only a few restaurant meals in America, he decided to turn it around and do something good with the money in Iran. Every year, he withdraws the pension and donates it to the needy. He has paid for surgeries, numerous medical treatments, eyeglasses, and medicine. About ten years ago, he met three children who had lost both parents and were living with their elderly grandparents. Every year, he supplies them with clothes, books, and toys. Before his last trip, he asked me if I could give him my laptop for the son. "I'm using it to write a book," I told him. "Give it to me when you're done," my father replied.

Last year, he bought desperately needed car parts for a man who makes his living as a driver and who without his car would have had no job. The year before, he paid for extensive repairs to a home inhabited by a family of nine. Luckily for them, my father did not have his Time-Life series with him.

Every year, my father returns to America with a suitcase full of pistachios and a head full of stories. He describes the luxuries of staying in a suite and ordering room service and making sure that the cleaning lady receives the biggest tip of her career. He tells me how odd it is for him to be treated with such fanfare in his own country and how everyone considers him to be such a big shot, all because of a pension that means almost nothing here.

After his last trip, I asked him if it was hard to return to America, where he is far from wealthy. "But, Firoozeh," he said, "I'm a rich man in America, too. I just don't have a lot of money."

Abadan, Iran, 1957. From left: my aunt Sedigeh;
my mother, pregnant with Farshid; my father; Mr. Modaress;
and my father's late uncle, Hassan.

ABOUT THE AUTHOR

FIROOZEH DUMAS graduated from the University of California at Berkeley. She lives with her husband and children in Northern California.